CAREER CHOICES
for Students of

HISTORY

by
CAREER ASSOCIATES

Walker and Company
NEW YORK

First published in the United States of America in 1985 by the Walker Publishing Company, Inc.

Published simultaneously in Canada by John Wiley & Sons Canada, Limited, Rexdale, Ontario.

Library of Congress Cataloging in Publication Data
Main entry under title:

Career choices for students of history.

Bibliography: p.
1. United States—Occupations. 2. College graduates—Employment—United States. 3. Vocational guidance—United States. I. Career Associates.
HF5382.5:U5C25545 1985 331.7'023 83-40447
ISBN 0-8027-0794-7
ISBN 0-8027-7254-4 (pbk.)

Printed in the United States of America

10 9 8 7 6 5 4 3 2 1

Titles in the Series

Career Choices for Students of:
Art
Business
Communications and Journalism
Computer Science
Economics
English
History
Mathematics
Political Science and Government
Psychology

Career Choices for Undergraduates Considering:
Law
An M.B.A.

Acknowledgments

We gratefully acknowledge the help of the many people who spent time talking to our research staff about employment opportunities in their fields. This book would not have been possible without their assistance. Our thanks, too, to Catalyst, which has one of the best career libraries in the country in its New York, NY, offices, and to the National Society for Internships and Experiential Education, Raleigh, NC, which provided information on internship opportunities for a variety of professions. The chapter on legal careers came about only through the excellent efforts of Lynn Stephens Strudler, Assistant Dean of the New York University School of Law Placement Office; special thanks, also, to the staff of researchers and interviewers who took time from their duties as law placement officers to gather the information in this chapter. The following individuals and organizations were particularly generous with their time and evaluations of the information contained in this book:

Marge Dover, National Association of Legal Assistants
Lynne Jones, Postgraduate Center for Mental Health
William Stolgitis, Society for Technical Communication

CAREER ASSOCIATES

CONTENTS

WHAT'S IN THIS BOOK FOR YOU?

BROADCASTING   1

    News   9
    Programming-Production   12
    Interviews   17

EDUCATION   21

    Teaching   27
    Interviews   33

GOVERNMENT   37

    The Peace Corps   41
    Intelligence Services   43
    The Foreign Service   45
    Interviews   52

HUMAN SERVICES   57

    Counseling   62
    Psychology Paraprofessional   63
    Administration   64
    Advocacy   65
    Research   66
    Community Relations   67
    Program Development   68
    Interviews   73

LAW   77

    Corporate Practice   80
    Government Service   84
    Private Practice   87

Other Areas of Practice   88
Interview   96

PARALEGAL PROFESSION   99

Interview   108

POLITICS   111

Legislative Staff   117
Campaigning   118
Public Interest Group Staff   122
Interviews   129

TECHNICAL WRITING   133

Writing and Editing   137
Interviews   142

BIBLIOGRAPHY   146

INDEX

WHAT'S IN THIS BOOK FOR YOU?

Recent college graduates, no matter what their major has been, too often discover that there is a dismaying gap between their knowledge and planning and the reality of an actual career. Possibly even more unfortunate is the existence of potentially satisfying careers that graduates do not even know about. Although advice from campus vocational counselors, family, friends, and fellow students can be extremely helpful, there is no substitute for a structured exploration of the various alternatives open to graduates.

The Career Choices Series was created to provide you with the means to conduct such an exploration. It gives you specific, up-to-date information about the entry-level job opportunities in a variety of industries relevant to your degree and highlights opportunities that might otherwise be overlooked. Through its many special features—such as sections on internships, qualifications, and working conditions—the Career Choices Series can help you find out where your interests and abilities lie in order to point your search for an entry-level job in a productive direction. This book cannot find you a job—only you can provide the hard work, persistence, and ingenuity that that requires—but it can save you valuable time and energy. By helping you to narrow the range of your search to careers that are truly suitable for you,d this book can help make hunting for a job an exciting adventure rather than a dreary—and sometimes frightening—chore.

The book's easy-to-use format combines general information about each of the industries covered with the hard facts that job-hunters must have. An overall explanation of each industry is followed by authoritative material on the job outlook for entry-level candidates, the competition for the openings that exist, and the new opportunities that may arise from such factors as expansion and technological development. There is a listing of employers by type and by geographic location and a sampling of leading companies by name—by no means all, but enough to give you a good idea of who the employers are.

The section on how to break into the field is not general how-to-get-a-job advice, but rather zeroes in on ways of getting a foot in the door of a particular industry.

You will find the next section, a description of the major functional areas within each industry, especially valuable in making your initial job choice. For example, communications majors aiming for magazine work can evaluate the editorial end, advertising space sales, circulation, or production. Those interested in accounting are shown the differences between management, government, and public accounting. Which of the various areas described offers you the best chance of an entry-level job? What career paths are likely to follow from that position? Will they help you reach your ultimate career goal? The sooner you have a basis to make the decision, the better prepared you can be.

For every industry treated and for the major functional areas within that industry, you'll learn what your duties—both basic and more challenging—are likely to be, what hours you'll work, what your work environment will be, and what range of salary to expect.* What personal and professional qualifications must you have? How can you move up—and to what? This book tells you.

You'll learn how it is possible to overcome the apparent contradiction of the truism, "To get experience you have to have experience." The kinds of extracurricular activities and work experience—summer and/or part-time—that can help you get and perform a job in your chosen area are listed. Internships are another way to get over that hurdle, and specific information is included for each industry. But you should also know that the directories published by the National Society for Internships and Experiential Education (Second Floor, 124 St. Mary's Street, Raleigh, NC 27605) are highly detailed and very useful. They are: *Directory of Undergraduate Internships, Directory of Washington Internships,* and *Directory of Public Service Internships.*

You'll find a list of the books and periodicals you should read to keep up with the latest trends in an industry you are considering, and the names and addresses of professional associations that can be helpful to you—through student chapters, open meetings, and

---

* Salary figures given are the latest available as the book goes to press.

printed information. Finally, interviews with professionals in each field bring you the experiences of people who are actually working in the kinds of jobs you may be aiming for.

Although your entry-level job neither guarantees nor locks you into a lifelong career path, the more you know about what is open to you, the better chance you'll have for a rewarding work future. The information in these pages will not only give you a realistic basis for a good start, it will help you immeasurably in deciding what to explore further on your own. So good reading, good hunting, good luck, and the best of good beginnings.

BROADCASTING

E VER since radio station KDKA started sending its programs to the general public in 1920 from a rooftop in Pittsburgh, broadcasting has become—and remains—the quickest and most widespread medium of mass communications. The country's 9000 radio stations and nearly 800 commercial television broadcast stations, plus public radio and television and cable TV, need a steady supply of employees willing to work long and hard, whether on the air, behind a desk, or out selling time in the business community. In both branches of the broadcast media, if you're not cut out for long hours, intense pressure, and teamwork, don't apply. A willingness to relocate, particularly in the early stages of your career, is another important consideration.

Most radio stations choose a particular segment of the population as their target audience and tailor all their programming to that group: news/talk; MOR (middle of the road, a mixture of news, talk, and music); religious; special music such as rock, country, jazz, or classical. It is estimated that 10 to 15 percent of radio stations are now completely automated, playing reels of tape-recorded music hour after hour—but they still require news-casts that are locally developed.

For political science or history majors, the most relevant area in commercial broadcasting is the news; but challenging opportunities can also be found in programming-production.

In the television industry, the networks, who were first on the scene, remain the giants of the industry, along with their local affiliates. Their job opportunities are the most coveted in the business. Independent stations rely primarily on old movies and syndicated reruns, but they still need talented news people. Public Broadcasting Service (PBS) stations have become an increasingly attractive career option for job-hunters because of the growing amount of station-generated programming, much of which gets national exposure through the PBS system.

In the last five years, as more and more homes were wired for cable television, opportunities have opened up for both experienced and inexperienced news reporters and anchors and production and programming staffers.

Graduates entering the broadcast field may have majored in any number of subjects. If your primary interest is news, a journalism degree is advisable, but a good political science or history background and an understanding of the political, social, and economic underpinnings of the news can be impressive. For most other jobs, employers want people who have demonstrated their interest in the medium through internships or summer jobs, or by independently developing, directing, or producing radio shows or video segments. Good reporting, writing, and editing skills and the ability to meet tight deadlines are essential.

Job Outlook

Job Openings Will Grow: As fast as average in radio; faster than average in TV.

Competition For Jobs: Keen

New Job Opportunities: In radio, the Federal Communications Commission (FCC) has recently dropped a variety of programming regulations to give stations much freer rein. An expected relaxing of other standards could mean the rise of as many as 1400 new FM stations in the next several years, and still more jobs will be created if the plan to expand the top end of the AM dial is put into effect.

In the meantime, look for new job opportunities at syndicated radio services, which provide and distribute a wide array of recorded materials and whose number keeps growing. The latest among these are the specialized networks, such as Hispanic News Service, headquartered in Washington, DC, and National Black Network, headquartered in New York, NY.

Low power television was recently approved by the FCC. These new stations will broadcast in a very limited geographic area and will be accessible to community and minority groups. They should be an excellent source of valuable entry-level experience, because their small staffs will allow individual members to try their hand at a variety of station functions.

Geographic Job Index

The corporate offices of both radio and TV networks are in New York, NY, and Los Angeles, CA. New York is the home of the news bureaus and most daytime soap operas, whereas the majority of network entertainment programming originates on the West Coast. Important network television desks also operate in Chicago, IL, and Washington, DC. However, most job openings exist outside these centers, in local broadcasting.

Who the Employers Are

MAJOR TELEVISION NETWORKS (ABC, CBS, NBC) employ thousands in their corporate offices, but job opportunities there are extremely limited for recent grads. An entry-level job at a network often requires the applicant to have professional experience or an advanced degree in business or law. Other jobs for recent graduates are usually secretarial or of the go-fer variety. Advancement is possible but difficult.

COMMERCIAL TELEVISION STATIONS operate across the country; there are approximately 780 such stations. The networks each have about 200 affiliates; some are directly owned by the parent network; others operate independently. In either case, each affiliate has its own hiring policies and procedures, as do the country's 180 independent stations.

NATIONAL RADIO NETWORKS (ABC, CBS, NBC) provide programming for their affiliate stations and, along with the other major networks—the Mutual Broadcasting System, AP Radio Network, UPI Audio, and RKO Radio Network—provide extensive coverage of national and international events and a variety of features to member stations.

STATE OR REGIONAL RADIO NETWORKS are associations of broadcast stations within a state or region that supply news of that area to member stations. These networks are the Florida News Network, Texas State Network, Oklahoma News Network, and the Arkansas, Georgia, Louisiana, Mississippi, and Missouri Networks.

The goal of many graduates is to land a job in one of the approximately 50 major television markets, which serve at least 500,000 viewing households, or the 25 largest U.S. cities that have a population of at least 1,300,000 and make up the major radio markets. Major market stations attract top-level, experienced people; competition for the relatively few entry-level jobs is intense.

MEDIUM AND SMALL MARKET RADIO STATIONS are located throughout the country. Cities with populations of between 500,000 and 1,000,000 are considered medium markets. Small market radio stations are found in communities of under 50,000, and nearly 40 percent of all radio stations in the United States fall into this latter category.

INDEPENDENT RADIO SYNDICATORS produce and distribute programming. Most of this production is music, but news, sports, and other features are also packaged. These services provide job opportunities primarily for graduates interested in programming and production.

PUBLIC TELEVISION STATIONS, numbering 300, make up the PBS system. They deliver educational, information, and artistic programming and operate in 49 states (all but Montana) and four U.S. territories, making PBS the world's most extensive television system. Each station does its own hiring, and staff size depends on the amount of production done at the station. However, very few public stations have the personnel or resources required for extensive production, so most PBS programming originates from the following five stations: WGBH (Boston, MA), WNET (New York, NY), WETA (Washington, DC), KCET (Los Angeles, CA), and WTTW (Chicago, IL). PBS headquarters in Washington, DC, is a small operation and employs primarily administrative staff. The radio counterpart of PBS is National Public Radio, with more than 180 stations across the United States. Here, too, hiring is done by individual stations, and programming is generated to the extent that station resources will allow. Other programming—such as NPR's "Morning Edition" and "All Things Considered"— comes from their Washington, DC, headquarters.

Major Employers

The eight largest U.S. television broadcast markets, those with more than 1,500,000 viewing households, are listed here in order of size. Each of these cities also has a number of independent stations in addition to the network affiliates and PBS stations listed below.

1. NEW YORK, NY
AFFILIATE: WABC (ABC), WCBS (CBS), WNBC
    (NBC)
PBS: WNET

2. LOS ANGELES, CA
AFFILIATE: KABC (ABC), KNBC (NBC), KNXT
    (CBS)
PBS: KCET, KLCS

3. CHICAGO, IL
AFFILIATE: WBBM (CBS), WLS (ABC), WMAQ
    (NBC)
PBS: WTTW

4. PHILADELPHIA, PA
AFFILIATE: KYW (NBC), WCAU (CBS), WPVI (ABC)
PBS: WHYY

5. SAN FRANCISCO, CA
AFFILIATE: KGO (ABC), KPIX (CBS), KRON (NBC)
PBS: KQED

6. BOSTON, MA
AFFILIATE: WBZ (NBC), WCBV (ABC), WNEV
    (CBS)
PBS: WGBH

7. DETROIT, MI
AFFILIATE: WDIV (NBC), WJBK (CBS), WXYZ
    (ABC)
PBS: WKAR, WTVS

8. WASHINGTON, DC
AFFILIATE: WDVM (CBS), WJLA (ABC), WRC
    (NBC)
PBS: WETA

The following cities are the top 25 radio markets, which each have
at least 1,300,000 listeners.

1. New York, NY
2. Los Angeles, CA
3. Chicago, IL
4. San Francisco, CA
5. Philadelphia, PA

6. Detroit, MI
7. Boston, MA
8. Houston, TX
9. Washington, DC
10. Dallas-Fort Worth, TX
11. Miami-Fort Lauderdale-Hollywood, FL
12. Naussau-Suffolk, Long Island, NY
13. St. Louis, MO
14. Pittsburgh, PA
15. Baltimore, MD
16. Seattle-Everett-Tacoma, WA
17. Minneapolis-St. Paul, MN
18. Atlanta, GA
19. Anaheim-Santa Ana-Garden Grove, CA
20. San Diego, CA
21. Cleveland, OH
22. Tampa-St. Petersburg, FL
23. Denver-Boulder, CO
24. Phoenix, AZ
25. Milwaukee-Racine, WI

How to Break into the Field

Knowing someone who can hire you or tell you about openings and recommend you is your best bet, but prior experience is the key. Investigate internship opportunities at a local station, or volunteer to work during summers and weekends. (Public television and radio stations are often the most receptive to volunteer help.) And get involved with your campus radio or TV station. Your best chance for a first job is at a small station. Send a carefully thought-out and well-written letter to the general manager of the station you've chosen and request an interview. Follow up with a phone call.

The once-rapid growth in programming services for the cable television industry slowed somewhat in 1983. Some services proved to be unprofitable and have folded or merged with more successful ones. Job openings, where they do occur, are often taken by experienced professionals. If you are willing to work part-time or as a free-lancer instead of waiting for a staff opening, you may stand a chance of finding a job in this area.

Most large radio stations hold newswriting examinations, which applicants have likened to taking the bar exam. The writer is given two hours to go over 12 hours' worth of wire copy and create a five-minute radio newscast from it. Such an exam should not be undertaken until you have a considerable amount of experience under your belt.

If you're female, or a member of a minority group, you can get help in finding positions in commercial broadcasting by writing to:

NAB Employment Clearinghouse
1771 N Street, N.W.
Washington, DC 20036

If you'd like to work in public radio, the National Association of Educational Broadcasters operates PACT (People and Careers in Telecommunications), a free, nationwide employment service. Write to:

National Association of Educational Broadcasters PACT
1346 Connecticut Avenue, N.W.
Washington, DC 20036

Competition for on-air jobs in both radio and television is intense. Hopefuls must have not only good reporting skills, but a clear speaking voice, an attractive appearance (for television), and an appealing presence as well. Starting in a small market is a must. Advancement comes by moving to larger and larger markets, and only the very best make it to the network level.

Much more plentiful are behind-the-scenes reporting jobs: writing and editing copy, preparing background research, and keeping and updating files on developing stories. These jobs can be just as exciting and demanding as those of reporters and anchors and provide better stepping-stones to management positions.

NEWS

By far the best opportunities for political science or history majors in broadcasting exist in radio and television news departments. The news department is often the largest at a station, but job opportunities are often awarded first to those with a journalism background. However, here your background may give you a competitive edge.

Radio news departments receive national and international news over a teletype machine from the news services: Associated Press (AP) and United Press International (UPI). Less frequently the news is sent as an audio feed by broadcast lines to local stations.

For local stories, the stations fend for themselves. Armed with a tape recorder and microphone, their reporters go wherever the action is. As a reporter, you'll interview people at the scene, take notes, and tape-record interviews and meetings before writing a story summarizing the event and editing the tape for appropriate quotes to thread into your story. You'll write, edit, and deliver the story back at the station if there's still time before the next newscast; otherwise you'll write the story on the spot and dictate it over the phone into a machine at the station.

Most radio stations broadcast the news at least once every hour. Although news jobs are extremely difficult to get, the total number of these jobs has increased because of the growing number of stations broadcasting all news 24 hours a day.

Qualifications

Personal: Natural curiosity. A capacity for hard work and long hours. Ability to handle pressure and deadlines. For on-air work, good diction. A voice and delivery that convey warmth and authority.

Professional: Television: Reporting and writing skills. Typing required; knowledge of video display terminals (VDTs) helpful, as these are becoming more common in TV newsrooms. Ability to work accurately with speed, usually under pressure of a deadline.

RADIO: Ability to write for the ear. Sound news judgment. Good reporting, editing, and rewriting skills. Ability to edit tape.

Career Paths

TELEVISION: (These apply primarily to off-camera personnel.)

LEVEL	JOB TITLE	EXPERIENCE NEEDED
Entry	Desk assistant	College degree
2	Newswriter	1-2 years
3	Assistant news producer	6-8 years
4	News producer	10-12 years

RADIO

LEVEL	JOB TITLE	EXPERIENCE NEEDED
Entry	Desk assistant, network radio Reporter, small network	College degree
2	Reporter, medium market	2 years
3	Reporter, major market News director, small market	5 years
4	News director, major market Reporter, network	10+ years

Job Responsibilities

Entry Level

THE BASICS: Clerical duties. Maintaining news service machines. Collecting and distributing audio feeds to news editors and writers. Helping prepare sports scores and weather round-ups. Checking facts. General messenger duties for the news department.

MORE CHALLENGING DUTIES: Television: Writing or rewriting copy. Simple editing of copy to conform to time limitations. Reviewing film clips. Radio: Interviewing sources. Putting together an early morning newscast by clearing the news wire machines of copy that has "moved" during the night and pulling stories for use on the upcoming newscasts, listening to audio feeds, phoning police and hospitals for overnight news and updates, then writing and editing the newscast from the material gathered.

Moving Up

As an assistant, you learn the daily routine of the newsroom, the style of its scripted copy, and the discipline to write under deadline. Once you reach the level of newswriter, you write the actual copy and you may edit other writers' stories. In radio, your next job will no doubt be reporting.

Several years of writing or reporting experience may lead to the position of assistant news producer in television, which combines organizational and managerial skills with critical judgment. In radio, a promotion possibility is becoming a news director, if you've proved yourself to be an ace reporter and, in addition, have managerial know-how. At most radio stations, the news director determines the overall news policy of the station, supervises the news personnel, and previews the newscasts to ensure that they're a satisfying blend of local, national, and international concerns. The news director also may serve as a reporter and newscaster.

In television, the assistant news producer, in cooperation with the news producer, oversees the daily routine, assigns stories, and decides which stories get precedence. These senior people also have the last word in the selection of accompanying film.

PROGRAMMING-PRODUCTION

Because the networks are responsible for the majority of daytime and evening programming, their program staffs number in the hundreds. Major programming areas beyond the news and documentary departments—sports, morning talk shows, soap operas, children's programs, and prime-time shows—have individual staffs. The television network programming and production staffs conceive, plan, and create most shows except for prime-time shows and made-for-TV movies, which they commission or purchase from independent production houses. In radio, all on-air material except for news is selected, prepared, or purchased by the programming department. Independent and network-affiliate TV stations still do a sizable amount of programming themselves, and this is where many job openings can be found. In radio, FCC regulations oblige the station to provide public service programming, and this may well be a place where your background is particularly apt. In addition, the surging popularity of talk shows has increased the number of people needed to plan and produce that type of programming. In fact, a growing number of major AM stations have become all-talk, and most stations do at least some talk show programming that is often aired early on Sunday mornings or late on Sunday evenings. Hosting a show, lining up guests, and developing a formula for talk programming is often the job of the director of public affairs. Although you may be given one of these responsibilities at a small station on your first job, you'll have to become more seasoned in programming before going on to a similar position at a medium or major market station.

Production staffers may develop program ideas, prepare scripts, work with free-lance writers and on-air talent, and edit the show after taping. In radio, if you're a talented behind-the-scenes programming person, you could be hired as an associate producer, helping the producer to conceive, develop, and produce a show; conducting interviews; writing scripts; and editing tapes. If you demonstrate taste and can forecast trends, you'll be ready to move up to producer, a position in which you'll choose the people to be interviewed, handle all the business arrangements, supervise production personnel, and act as overall manager of the program. Success in any of these areas may land you a job as program director, responsible for coordinating and presenting the complete daily programming schedule.

The television production assistant is, in many ways, an apprentice. Opportunities for advancement depend on the size of the station and the complexity of its operations. As assistant producer, you might work on a specific regular program or on various specials. You typically then become a producer, working in ever larger markets on more involved programming. Or you might move on to an administrative position, such as production director or program director.

ADDITIONAL INFORMATION

Salaries

Network people make the highest salaries. At both independent and network-affiliated stations, the larger the market, the higher the pay. Those who work in public television or radio make less than their counterparts at commercial stations. The following figures, compiled by the National Association of Broadcasters in a 1983 survey, represent the average salary nationwide.

RADIO

News editor	$15,250
News reporter	$15,294
News announcer	$15,320
News director	$19,385

TELEVISION

News reporter	$20,497
News producer	$37,558
News anchor	$42,348

Working Conditions

Hours: Radio: Many radio stations operate 24 hours a day, seven days a week, so in news expect to work long hours. As a neophyte, you'll often be assigned the worst shifts (midnight to 8 A.M.; 4:30 A.M. to noon), and to weekend and holiday assignments. Be prepared for overtime. Television: News must be reported up until the end of the 11 P.M. newscast seven days a week, and into the early hours on the networks' late-night programs.

Environment: In general, the atmosphere is noisy, cluttered, and hectic, with ringing phones and loud talk. Office privacy is a luxury reserved for senior staff members. Because reporters are under continuous deadline pressure, it's a high-tension, fast-moving atmosphere.

Workstyle: As a reporter, you're on your feet and out of the office much of the day, tracking down stories. The rest of the time you're in the newsroom editing and rewriting stories that come in over the wires.

Travel: Only network-level reporters do a significant amount of out-of-town travel, and they are usually based in major cities or even abroad.

Extracurricular Activities/Work Experience

Campus newspaper, publications, radio or television
station—reporting and writing, production,
announcing

Volunteer—local public radio or television station

Sports events—announcing

Drama club—directing, acting, technical crew

Debate club—participant

Internships

The International Radio and Television Society's internship program is open only to junior and senior communications majors. Investigate summer and part-time opportunities by contacting local radio and television stations and cable systems. Although some stations pay interns, most take them only as volunteers.

Recommended Reading

BOOKS

Anchorwoman by Jessica Savitch, Berkeley Publishing: 1983

Before the Colors Faded by Harry Reasoner, Quill Publications: 1983

Broadcasting Yearbook published by Broadcasting Publications, Inc. (lists names and addresses of radio stations, national and regional networks, and major program producers)

Good Evening Everybody by Lowell Thomas, Avon Books: 1977

Larry King by Larry King and Emily Yoffe, Simon & Schuster: 1982

The Making of a Woman Reporter: This Is Judy Woodruff at the White House by Judy Woodruff and Kathy Maxa, Addison-Wesley Publishing Company: 1982

Not So Wild a Dream by Eric Severeid, Atheneum Publishers: 1978

On the Radio: With Harden and Weaver by Frank Harden, et al., William Morrow and Company: 1983

Over the Wire and on TV: CBS and UPI in Campaign '80 by Michael J. Robinson, Russel Sage Foundation: 1983

Radio in the Television Age by Peter Fornatale and Joshua Mills, Overlook Press: 1983

Television Digest's Cable and Station Coverage Atlas, Revised, TV and Cable Factbook: 1982

PERIODICALS

Billboard (weekly), Billboard Publications, 1 Astor Plaza, 1515 Broadway, New York, NY 10036

Broadcasting (weekly), Broadcasting Publications, Inc., 1735 DeSales Street, N.W., Washington, DC 20036
Cable Age (biweekly), Television Editorial Corporation, 1270 Avenue of the Americas, New York, NY 10020

Cable Television Business (weekly), Cardiff Publishing Company, 6430 Yosemite Street, Englewood, CO 80111

Inside TV (monthly), McFadden-Bartell Corporation, 215 Lexington Avenue, New York, NY 10016

Radio & Records (weekly), 1930 Century Park West, Los Angeles, CA 90067

Television Radio Age (biweekly), 1270 Avenue of the Americas, New York, NY 10020

Variety (weekly), Variety, Inc., 154 West 46th Street, New York, NY 10036

Professional Associations

American Women in Radio and Television
1321 Connecticut Avenue, N.W.
Washington, DC 20036

International Radio and Television Society
420 Lexington Avenue
New York, NY 10170

The National Association of Broadcasters
1771 N Street, N.W.
Washington, DC 20036

The National Radio Broadcasters Association
1705 DeSales Street, N.W.
Washington, DC 20036

INTERVIEWS

Mark Scheerer, Age 34
Roving Correspondent
ABC Radio News, New York, NY

Although I majored in journalism in college, I never took a broadcasting course. I didn't even work at the campus radio station. I was too shy to speak in front of a microphone—or so I thought until I got my first job at a small FM station in Sylvania, Ohio. I worked as a disc jockey and a news broadcaster there before I was named news director for a larger station, WIOT, in Ohio.

As news director at major stations in Cincinnati, Philadelphia, and Chicago, I've covered five national political conventions, White House news conferences, the emergency at Three Mile Island, the visits of the Pope, the Winter Olympics, the World Series, and the Super Bowl.

For several years, I worked the morning drive shift (6 to 10 A.M.). It's difficult to be creative, funny, and compelling on the air at an early hour. But that's the time when most people want their daily dose of news. When you have to get up at four o'clock in the morning, your social life is terrible.

It took me 11 years to land the radio job of my dreams—working as a roving correspondent for ABC News—but it was worth it. Had I been tied down with a relationship or marriage, I might not have been able to relocate as often as I did, which is what most people in my business do in order to move up to bigger and better markets.

I think I have the greatest job in radio news—I go wherever a big story or event is happening, and I get to tell it to hundreds of thousands of young Americans. While most of the stories I work on are exciting, I'm also required to be on the scene whenever necessary, which may mean showing up at 8 A.M. to cover a story on dioxin contamination in Hoboken, New Jersey.

If you want to work in radio, get as much firsthand experience as you can while you're still in school—at the campus station or a local one. Take a wide variety of courses so you're knowledgeable about many subjects. And be persistent in your search to get into a radio news slot. It's competitive, but if you're willing to start out at a small station and build on your experience, you're bound to go places.

John Carver, Age 41
Director of Grant Support
WGBH Public Television, Boston, MA

The highlights of my job are selling a quality product and working with people who really enjoy their work. I'm surrounded by very bright people who want to be here. There's a team spirit at WGBH that I have never known on other jobs.

I'm responsible for finding corporate sponsors or underwriters for programs my station produces for national delivery through PBS. My clients are high-level corporate people, usually close to senior vice presidential level. To them, I'm not so much a salesman as I am a broker, bringing two interested parties together. My job is to travel to cities where corporate headquarters are located to see if I can interest them in associating their names with a production. Usually, their company has expressed interest in public television, and my job is to find the right product for them. I talk frequently with our programming department to try to match up something that's in the works with a particular company's needs.

I like to define our product as the Rolls-Royce of TV programming. Those of us in public television see ourselves as part of a widely accepted alternative to standard and predictable commercial fare. We make less money than our counterparts in network or local TV. But in my department, there's more opportunity than in others to earn a good living because we're paid on a salary plus commission basis.

EDUCATION

MANY of the world's most prominent citizens have either started their careers as teachers or have added teaching to the list of their accomplishments. Leonardo da Vinci, Leo Tolstoy, Henry Kissinger, and Jimmy Carter are but a few.

Through the ages the theory of education has fascinated many. Tolstoy put off writing his novels in order to work out his ideas about education, and Plato devoted many of his philosophical treatises to exploring how knowledge is transmitted from teacher to student. People teach, he said, not by writing books or making speeches, but by becoming vitally involved in dialogue, in human relationships. Teaching is something that happens between two people; it is communication, knowledge passing from one to another.

Thousands of years later this still holds true. Ask almost any teacher what constitutes good teaching and he or she will tell you: good teaching is caring for the people you teach. There are less altruistic reasons for becoming a teacher, however, and if you ask a veteran, he or she will probably start with summer vacation—not to mention the three or four weeks of holidays that can accumulate at Christmas, Easter, Thanksgiving, and the scattered celebrations of America's heroes.

Teaching can often serve personal interests, too. For those who love to act, teaching provides the perfect audience. For those who like to be in charge, teaching is one of the few professions where you start off as the boss. For scholars, teaching is a way to delve further into your favorite subjects.

Of course, teaching is not the ideal state. Although the starting salaries can be commensurate with the job market as a whole, salaries for experienced teachers most definitely are not. Crime in the schools has received a lot of national coverage, but what is called crime by the media usually means discipline problems in the school, such as absenteeism, vandalism, and abuse of drugs or alcohol. But prospective teachers must take into account the disciplinary difficulties some of them will encounter.

Perhaps the most troubling problem facing a person interested in a teaching career is the beating teachers' reputations have taken in the last decade. As the quality of education seems to have gone steadily downward, largely because of factors beyond teachers' control, teachers themselves have had to take on more and more responsibilities—not only in the area of teaching, but in the area of genuine care and concern for their students.

Few professions, however, have more social significance than teaching, and none offers the sense of satisfaction that comes from contributing directly and positively to a young person's future. When Wally Schirra, one of the original seven U.S. astronauts, was asked who was the most influential person in his life, he didn't hesitate to say his second-grade teacher.

As computers become standard equipment in more and more classrooms, teacher applicants with computer skills are in a better position to be hired. The educational value of computers, however, depends on how teachers use them. The computer can be used as an automated taskmaster or, more importantly, as an interactive device. Some programs teach sophisticated skills such as thinking and writing even to very small children. Computers can grab and keep a student's attention, stimulate, and motivate him or her to higher levels of achievement. But it is still up to the teacher to provide the crucial interaction that makes learning possible.

Job Outlook

Job Openings Will: Decline

Competition For Jobs: Keen

New Job Opportunities: If current migration trends continue, a 25% decline in the number of 15 to 19-year-olds is projected in the northeast and north central states between 1980 and 1990. The rate of decline is expected to be 15% in the rest of the country. These statistics, combined with the fact that the 61,650 secondary school teacher applicants from the graduating class of 1981 exceeded the number of job openings by 18,150, indicate that new job opportunities are not plentiful. These statistics do not take into account, however, the graduates who applied for and subsequently accepted positions with independent schools.

Because of the recent budget cuts, school systems have suffered severe cutbacks in expenditures in all areas including teacher hiring and salary increases. But positions do exist, especially in math and computer sciences. Many teachers retire, leave the profession, or find administrative positions, creating thousands of openings each year. Willingness to relocate increases their chances of finding a position.

In 1978 a law was passed mandating special education for all handicapped children. The number of special education teachers rose more than 30 percent between 1970 and 1980, to 187,900. The Department of Education is still predicting a shortage of special ed teachers as the population of children needing special education continues to grow. Job supply is not the only incentive for entering this area; generally, special ed teachers are paid anywhere from $500 to $2000 more per year than other teachers.

Many parents are turning to church-affiliated institutions for the education of their children. Although salaries are almost always lower, job prospects in this area will grow.

New opportunities also exist in the areas of continuing education and preschool education. Adult education courses on virtually every subject imaginable are taught all over the country at local libraries and community centers. The need for nursery schools, some operated by teachers from their own homes, is growing as more and more mothers of young children work full- or part-time.

Geographic Job Index

The majority of jobs are found in suburban school systems and city schools; fewer positions are available in rural and remote regions. New York, California, Texas, Pennsylvania, Michigan, and Illinois have the greatest teacher populations and the greatest number of new openings for teachers. Since the southwestern and mountain states are growing considerably in population and school enrollments are on the rise, the need for teachers in those areas is growing at a faster rate than anywhere else in the country.

Who the Employers Are

PUBLIC SCHOOLS
Secondary positions: 925,000
Elementary positions: 1,175,000

PRIVATE SCHOOLS
Secondary positions: 93,000
Elementary positions: 184,000

California leads the country in the number of private schools with 2444. Of these, 1574 are under the auspices of a religious organization. New York, with 1923, comes in second; 1504 of these schools are church-affiliated.

How to Break into the Field

Teacher certification requirements vary according to state and are always handled by the state's department of education. The best way to find out how to be certified in a given state is to seek advice from the education department of your college. Many schools of education are members of the National Council of Accreditation of Teacher Education, and graduates of these schools are most likely to be certifiable in every state. Certain education requirements are necessary for teaching in public schools; for teaching in public or most private high schools, you are also required to have majored in the subject in which you wish to teach. Private elementary and high schools usually do not require either certification or education courses.

College placement offices provide the most information and the best service in the quest for a teaching position. Local school systems keep them informed of openings, and more distant job opportunities can be found on their bulletin boards as well. Information can also be found in the classified sections of local newspapers.

An interesting cover letter and résumé addressed to a principal will usually produce a response or an application form. Visiting the community in which you want to find a job can produce contacts and word of mouth recommendations.

Personal recommendations are always a good way to secure a job, particularly in an independent school. Application to an independent school is made to the headmaster through a letter of introduction, and a résumé that should include any extracurricular activities that would make you a more valuable staff member. The best time to apply is in the fall before the year in which you wish to be employed. Hiring decisions are usually made in March or April.

To save time and gather information about out-of-town schools, it can be useful to contact national placement organizations.

Among these are:

North American Educational Consultants
P.O. Box 995
Barre, VT 05641
802-479-0157
(specializes in secondary schools here and abroad)

Careers in Education
P.O. Box 455
East Stroudsburg, PA 18301

Independent Education Services
80 Nassau Street
Princeton, NJ 08540
800-257-5102 (toll free) or 609-921-6195
(specializes in placing prospective private school
    teachers)

Independent Educational Counselors Association
P.O. Box 125
Forest, MA 02644
(specializes in independent schools for the learning
    disabled)

International Job Opportunities

Opportunities to teach abroad in a variety of subject areas are available to elementary and secondary school teachers through a program sponsored by the United States Information Agency. An applicant must have at least a bachelor's degree, be a United States citizen, and have three years of successful full-time teaching experience, preferably in the subject and at the level for which an application is made. Information and application materials may be obtained from:

Teacher Exchange Branch
United States Information Agency
301 Fourth Street, S.W.
Washington, DC 20547

Opportunities to teach abroad aren't limited to those with three years of teaching experience. For example, speaking Russian can lead you to be sponsored by the American Field Service to participate in an exchange program with the Soviet Union. The Peace Corps, the National Education Association, and UNESCO all offer opportunities for teachers abroad. The most comprehensive brochure on the subject, *Study and Teaching Opportunities Abroad* by Pat Kern McIntyre, can be obtained from the U.S. Department of Education, Washington, DC 20402.

TEACHING

Qualifications

Personal: A genuine desire to work with and care for young people. Ability to lead a group. Strong character. Stamina. Creativity. Well organized.

Professional: College degree. For public schools, certification as well. High school teachers are usually required to have majored in the subject they choose to teach. For elementary school teaching you need a broad range of knowledge and interests, including some instinct for children and how they develop.

Career Paths

LEVEL	JOB TITLE	EXPERIENCE NEEDED
Entry	Teacher	College degree; certification as required
1	Teacher (with master's)	Master's degree in education or in subject area
3	Department Head (high school)	7-10 years

Job Responsibilities

Entry Level

THE BASICS: Presenting subject matter. Developing lesson plans. Preparing and giving examinations. Arranging class and individual projects that contribute to the learning process. Attending parent conferences, field trips, and faculty meetings. In junior and senior high schools, homeroom guidance, study hall supervision.

MORE CHALLENGING DUTIES: Club leadership. Sports coach or leading support for sports activities. Directing activities in which the entire school participates, such as assemblies or fund raisers.

Moving Up

Opportunities for advancement exist in the field of education, especially for those with energy, ideas, and the ability to communicate with both adults and children. Administrators, principals, and superintendents can earn up to $45,000 per year and have a major influence on the communities they serve. To move into administrative or supervisory positions, you must have one year of graduate education, several years of classroom experience, and sometimes a special certificate, depending on the state.

The concept of master teacher is a new one, but school systems in Texas are already awarding teachers who achieve this level—by virtue of experience and effectiveness—with greater responsibility, status and a significant increase in pay. High school teachers have the opportunity to become department heads.

Good and creative teachers with some years of experience are in an excellent position to become educational consultants either as editors of textbooks, directors of special programs, or within the school system as curriculum developers. Especially in the areas of math and the sciences, experienced teachers are being pulled from the classroom to teach other teachers.

To move up in the field of education, you have to have the ability to deal with all kinds of people in all kinds of sensitive situations.

You must have a dedication to the job that continues long after school's over. And you must show a willingness to continue your own education, gaining a master's degree or even a doctoral degree in education or in your subject area.

Teaching can also be a springboard into other professions. Businesses have long known that the experience one gets as a teacher is excellent training for executive positions in marketing, public relations, and advertising. The analytical skills that teachers develop in the classroom, as well as the ability to deal with many different people at many different levels, cannot be taught in a business school. These skills that teachers use day in and day out can be effectively transferred to the business world.

ADDITIONAL INFORMATION

Salaries

Teachers progress in salary as they gain experience. Salaries vary widely from state to state. Starting annual salaries can range from $10,000 to $16,000, but generally higher salaries are to be found in the suburban areas. According to the National Educational Association, for secondary and elementary teachers, in 1982-83, the state with the highest average annual salary was Alaska at $33,953. Washington, DC, came in second with an average salary of $26,045. The lowest paying states were Mississippi, with $14,285; Arkansas, with $15,176; and Vermont, with $15,338.

The salary of an independent secondary school teacher is not commensurate with that of a public school teacher, although there are fringe benefits that can often compensate for the difference in pay. At boarding schools, teachers can expect to receive free room and board or rent-reduced housing on or near campus. Travel expenses and smaller workloads also help to compensate for smaller salaries.

Working Conditions

Hours: Most teachers spend between six and seven hours a day with 15 to 30 children, but that is far from the end of the day. Experienced teachers can often get by with a quick review of their old lesson plans, but new teachers should anticipate an extra two or three hours a day for preparation and correction. Some of the work can be done during the summer vacation and the three or four weeks of holiday during the year.

Environment: This can range from the rolling hills of a rural boarding school to the bleak insides of an inner-city school. Teachers can have access to tennis courts, swimming pools, even a stable full of horses, or they may have to content themselves, for recreation, with the smoke-filled faculty room.

The classroom environment is generally what you make it. Elementary teachers can plaster their walls with children's art, waxed leaves in fall, cutouts of flowers in spring. In secondary schools, decoration can be anything from a chart of chemical elements to a poster of the rock star of the moment.

Workstyle: Most classrooms consist of a blackboard, a big desk, and 20 or 30 smaller ones facing front. Yet each teacher has the choice to make each class either student-centered or teacher-centered. Some teachers prefer to lecture or read to their students; other promote student discussion to various degrees. History teachers have discovered that role-playing and mini-dramas can give life to an epoch. English classes can concentrate on grammar, literature, or writing. With the availability of computers, students are less likely to tune out of math class because of the possibilities for direct interaction and feedback. The art room can offer the freest environment. Many teachers turn on music while students paint or sculpt, and students chat among themselves or with the teacher as they work. The major environmental factor in any class will always be the moods and attitudes of the students, and this is where the good teacher becomes the chief architect of his or her surroundings.

Travel: If travel is your end, teaching abroad can be your means. Class trips and outings are also available to the enterprising teacher. Schools will often pay the expenses of a teacher attending a conference, chaperoning a team to an out-of-town match, or accompanying students to recreational activities.

Extracurricular Activities/Work Experience

Volunteer—Big Brother/Sister program, tutoring, sports, summer camps, teen counseling, child care centers for retarded or culturally disadvantaged children

Athletics—sports (participation can lead to coaching positions in secondary schools)

School—cheerleading, debate society, literary clubs, student newspapers, yearbook publications, student government, drama club, glee club, art club, alumni/admissions administrative work

Internships

Aside from the student teaching that accompanies college or graduate certification and degree programs, there are few opportunities for teaching internships, except at a limited number of independent schools. They offer the opportunity to get experience in teaching without taking on the responsibility of a full-time teacher. Under the tutelage of a head teacher, the intern learns the ins and outs of the profession. Both school and intern benefit from such a program and the intern is often paid a nominal salary. Contact individual independent schools to see if they have a program.

Recommended Reading

BOOKS

Don't Smile Until Christmas: Accounts of the First Year of Teaching, Kevin Ryan, ed. University of Chicago Press: 1970

The Teacher Rebellion by David Selden, Howard University Press: 1970

Teaching School: Points Picked Up by Eric Johnson, Walker & Company: 1979

PERIODICALS

Academic Journal: The Educator's Employment Magazine (biweekly), Box 392, Newton, CT 06470

American Education (ten times a year), U.S. Department of Education, 400 Maryland Avenue, S.W., Washington, DC 20202

Arithmetic Teacher/Mathematics Teacher (ten times a year), 11906 Association Drive, Reston, VA 22091

The Association for School, College and University (ASCUS) Staffing Annual: A Job Search Handbook for Educators (annual), Box 411, Madison, WI 53711

Chronicle of Higher Education (weekly), 1333 New Hampshire Avenue, N.W., Washington, DC 20036

Harvard Educational Review (quarterly), Graduate School of Education, Harvard University, 13 Appian Way, Cambridge, MA 02138

Today's Education (quarterly), National Education Association, 1201 Sixteenth Street, N.W., Washington, DC 20036

Professional Associations

American Federation of Teachers
11 Dupont Circle, N.W.
Washington, DC 20036

Association for School, College and University Staffing
ASCUS Office
Box 411
Madison, WI 53711

National Education Association
1201 Sixteenth Street, N.W.
Washington, DC 20036

INTERVIEWS

Margaret Thompson, Age 39
Secondary School Teacher
Needham High School and Newman Middle School, Needham,
    MA

Although the competition for ~~English~~ *History* teaching positions is very
fierce now, in five or ten years there should be a real market. If
you're lucky enough to find a position right now, though, it can be
the most rewarding experience of your life.

There's autonomy. You're your own boss. Once you're in that
classroom, the door is shut. You can be amazingly creative. Every
single day is a new challenge. And you get to show off a lot.
Probably more than any other subject, teaching ~~English~~ *History* calls on
you to perform. *History*

Teaching ~~English~~ is like conducting an orchestra. You're in
charge, but the students have to play their own instruments. The
more they play their instruments, the happier they are. And when

they can hear those instruments being played together in an orchestra it gives them a big thrill.

For example, sixth and seventh graders are being introduced to literature for the first time in their lives; you teach them about the components of a story—the climax, the development, the resolution; then they read the story and for the first time have a sense of recognition; they're reading about characters who are experiencing some of the same conflicts they are. They listen to each other's interpretations and all of a sudden they don't feel alone anymore.

I think literature is one of the most subtle ways of affecting people's lives. You have to know how to choose the literature that will be the catalyst to self-understanding and give students the structural tools to explore their own lives.

What kind of person would really have fun teaching? A caring person. One who enjoys stroking and being stroked. I've been teaching for 13 years now. I'm making about maximum salary, $26,000 a year. But the feeling of loving more than balances the salary. I'll never stop teaching. It's a joy.

Laura Daigen, Age 29
Fourth-Grade Teacher
New York, NY

I started out teaching Spanish in a high school, but I decided there was a lot more good to be done as a bilingual elementary teacher. I was somewhat disillusioned with the politics of the school where I worked. Teachers who had been there longer made sure that they had no problem students in their classes and that kids with low test scores were taught by the rookies. The Spanish language textbooks were poor and antiquated in their absence of girls and women.

When you're working in a public school in the inner city, the needs of your kids are infinite. There's very little support from the administration or cohesiveness among the faculty. You're alone with kids who have more emotional needs than you can deal with. There is no one to help you help them.

Even under the best of conditions, the hours are long. Sometimes I'm there until six or seven and I'm not the last one to leave. I'm making plans for new curriculum, I'm marking papers, I'm cleaning up the room. You're never finished when you're a teacher: you dream it, you go to sleep thinking about it, and you wake up thinking about it. You're teaching eleven pieces of curriculum and you have to coordinate them and give enough time to each one. It was easier teaching Spanish in a high school, because I was teaching one subject at three different levels and the students had the responsibility of absorbing what you gave them. But when you're teaching elementary school and the kid isn't learning, it's your fault.

If someone were trying to decide whether or not to go into teaching, the first question I would ask him or her is: Do you like kids? Are you ready to take on the responsibility of little human beings and their emotional needs? There is tremendous satisfaction in watching children grow, seeing them move out of themselves and being able to give; recognizing their right to receive fair treatment knowing they can effect change if they see an injustice being done. It feels great to have a kid say, "I like math this year," or "I don't have to try to read these books, I can just read them," or to see kids take charge of their own lives and take pride in what they've done on their own.

I think what makes a good teacher is the sincerity of his or her commitment—whatever it is. It can be to help children love reading or to help them see themselves as important pieces of society or to help them realize the value of their own ethnicity. It has to be more than a vague "I love kids"—but you have to love kids, too.

No matter what I end up doing with my life, I'll always be able to look back on these five or six years and say those were years that I spent doing what I really wanted to do. Perhaps I haven't been well-compensated economically, but the job is rewarding. I will always be able to say that I did something that was meaningful, something that helped others.

GOVERNMENT

SETTING aside any judgment on the controversy about the size of government—is it too big, or not big enough?—the simple fact is that today government is the single largest employer in the United States. Millions work for federal, state, and local governments in an endless variety of jobs. Virtually every profession and trade found in the private and nonprofit sectors are found in the public sector. Whatever your skills and interests, and whatever profession you have chosen to pursue, a place may be waiting for you in government service.

For many people, government is more than an employer, it is a career choice in itself. They find government service appealing because they know that their efforts contribute to the nation, the state, or the community. On the less idealistic side, many government jobs, particularly those at the federal level, offer excellent opportunities for on-the-job training. Often, you can move quickly into a management position. Government also offers exceptional benefits and job security.

The skills of the history major are in demand in many government positions. The Smithsonian Institution, the National Archives, state archives, museums and historical societies, and other governement-managed cultural institutions employ historians, archivists, curators, and individuals with training in historic preservation. The majority of these openings, particularly in the better-known institutions, are filled by applicants with advanced degrees. With a bachelor's degree, you have the best chance of using your education by working for a state or local government. The competition is fierce, so you must have a superior academic record and some work experience.

Government also provides a number of other unique personal and career opportunities not found elsewhere. Three opportunities with the federal government that should be of special interest to the history major are:

- **The Peace Corps**
- **Intelligence Services**
- **Foreign Service**

If you are intrigued by any of these, begin your investigation early in your academic career. Each is highly selective and requires specific skills and experience. You must be well-prepared by the time you graduate in order to compete.

Job Outlook

Job Openings Will Grow: More slowly than average

Competition For Jobs: Keen

Government hiring policies at the local, state, and federal levels are affected by political decisions. By decree or legislative action, a new department, agency, or bureau may be created, an established organization eliminated, or existing offices merged. Since 1980, a strong movement against big government has produced hiring freezes throughout the federal government. The greatest need is for individuals with advanced degrees (computer science, biology, health, and agricultural specialties, among others) and in clerical positions. Neither option is suited for those with undergraduate degrees. White-collar entry-level job openings are limited or nonexistent in most departments (the Department of Defense is a notable exception, but even it is not hiring extensively). Although attitudes and politics may change, the simple fact remains that there is a glut of federal employees. To ease the situation, the jobs of many individuals who leave government service are not being refilled.

But as job opportunities dwindle at the federal level, they are growing at the state and local levels. As Washington, DC, requires these governmental bodies to provide services once handled by federal agencies, administrative and managerial positions are being created.

Geographic Job Index

The Washington, DC, metropolitan area has the highest concentration of federal jobs. Most federal departments and agencies are headquartered either in the city itself or in the Virginia-Maryland suburbs. However, federal offices are spread across the United States. Some offices, such as the Internal Revenue Service and the Federal Bureau of Investigation, are found in every state; others, such as the State Department and the National Archives, have branches in key cities. Military installations often create high numbers of nonmilitary jobs in the areas around them. When applying to the federal government, relocation is an important consideration. Your willingness to move may increase your chances of winning a coveted position.

At the state and local levels, you will find the highest concentrations of jobs in state capitals, county seats and large cities.

How to Break into the Field

Unlike many other employers, the federal government offers a great deal of aid to job-hunters, but because you are dealing with a bureaucracy, red-tape hassles are unavoidable. Be prepared to be aggressive, assertive, and, above all, patient in your job search.

The place to begin is a federal job information office (check the Yellow Pages for the nearest location). Here you can learn about the various jobs within the federal government, as well as the current hiring outlook. The information centers have publications called occupational briefs, each of which describes a job in detail. These brochures are also available at libraries, but only at an information center are you sure to get the most recent information.

You should first determine if the position you seek is within the competitive service or the excepted service. Jobs in the competitive service are handled through the federal government's central personnel agency, the Office of Personnel Management. Departments and agencies that hire under the excepted service have their own personnel departments. In either case, you file a basic application called Standard Form 171 and submit an academic transcript. Some departments require additional procedures— written tests, security checks, medical exams, and others. Your qualifications are evaluated and you are given a numerical rating and placed on a register. When your name appears at the top of the register, your application is submitted to offices that are hiring. If you have not noted any geographic restrictions, you could be considered by any potential federal employer anywhere in the country. You may be interviewed in person or, if the office is distant, over the phone.

An application may be renewed each year by reporting all pertinent work experience. Although work experience can give you an edge over other candidates, a career in government should be started within a few years after graduation. The federal government prefers to promote from within. An outside (or "non status") person will be hired for a management position instead of a government ("status") employee only if the position requires very specific skills.

There are U.S. Government Offices of Personnel Management in Washington, DC, Atlanta, GA, Boston, MA, Chicago, IL, Dallas, TX, Denver, CO, New York, NY, Philadelphia, PA, St. Louis, MO, San Francisco, CA, and Seattle, WA.

State and local governments also have personnel departments. The hiring process may be similar to that of the federal government, but should be less complicated.

Again, the first step is to find out where job information is available and to whom applications must be addressed. Many state and local governments require that their employees reside in the political division, which could be an important consideration in your job search.

International Job Opportunities

In addition to obvious international jobs, such as the foreign service and the Peace Corps, the federal government offers a number of opportunities to work abroad. The Office of Personnel Management and Federal Job Information Centers have information on the types of overseas jobs available and the qualifications. In many instances, competence in a foreign language is preferred or required. (Keep in mind that a large number of these international opportunities are for clerical personnel.)

THE PEACE CORPS

More than 5000 Americans work as Peace Corps volunteers in the developing nations of Africa, Asia, Latin America, and the Pacific. They work on an endless variety of projects—starting a chicken farm, building a road system, working in hospitals, or with youth. Americans of any age and background can apply, and many are recent college graduates. All offer their skills as volunteers, making two-year commitments, and serve as guests of the host countries. You may work on projects funded by the United States government, or you may receive funds from other governments or international agencies. You may work with other volunteers—either from the Peace Corps or from other organizations, including non-American ones—or you may be sent on an assignment alone.

Service in the Peace Corps does not mark the beginning of a set career path. Some former volunteers work as administrators with the Peace Corps, but no one serves with this purpose in mind. Instead, individuals apply because of the extraordinary experiences offered. Your courage, endurance, and creativity and your managerial, organizational, and interpersonal skills are tested in situations completely unlike any you have known. You become a friend, teacher, and partner to the people you work with, adapting to their culture and living in the same surroundings. You may find yourself in an isolated mountain village or on a remote South Sea island, surrounded by people who have had limited exposure to Americans. You may have to contend with some resentment to outside intrusion, and you risk your personal safety by living with primitive sanitation and health facilities.

Although the personal rewards should be your primary concern, Peace Corps experience can be a valuable asset if you plan a career in the international sector, whether that career is the foreign service, the United Nations (although opportunities for United States citizens are extremely limited there), or other international organizations, or in international business. It is equally valuable if you plan to teach, do research, or write about global affairs. The experience can also enhance advanced studies in Third World politics, international relations, or global economics.

Applicants are carefully screened by former volunteers. Good intentions are not enough; you should be able to demonstrate some skills in agriculture, construction, nutrition, business, science, or health and community service. Volunteers receive 8 to 12 weeks of training in the United States, which can include a crash course in native language and customs. Usually, volunteers are sent to host countries in groups; however, chances are good that once you arrive you will not be working with other volunteers. You may start a project from scratch, or work in established institutions, such as schools and hospitals.

During your two-year commitment, you receive a modest living allowance, transportation to and from your assignment, and a small compensation (presently $175 per month) that is given you on your return.

For application information, write:
The Peace Corps
806 Connecticut Avenue, N.W.
Washington, DC 20526

INTELLIGENCE SERVICES

The cloak-and-dagger intrigues of spying have given way to satellite photography and reams of computer-generated statistics. The secret agent still serves a purpose, but twentieth-century intelligence gathering has evolved from Mata Hari to modern science. The federal government employs large staffs of skilled people with varied backgrounds, all of whom endeavor to analyze and understand the current world situation.

The two main sources of intelligence gathering for the United States government are the Central Intelligence Agency (CIA) and the less well-known Defense Intelligence Agency (DIA). The CIA reports directly to the president and the National Security Council, providing information on the world situation as it relates to national security. The DIA also investigates international matters, but is responsible for providing information directly to the Department of Defense. Although it serves the military, DIA analysts are nonmilitary personnel. In many respects, both organizations analyze the same data, but the users of this information and their purposes in requesting it are different.

The DIA closely monitors foreign military affairs. The agency assesses the strength and preparedness of foreign armed forces, the types and quantities of their equipment, the movement of these forces, and the new weapons they develop. To complement its understanding of military affairs, the DIA investigates the history, politics, economics, geography, industrial capability, and resources of a nation. This agency keeps up-to-date information on foreign military installations, tracks compliance with international arms agreements, and will, if necessary, investigate the status of prisoners of war and answer questions about those missing in action.

The DIA has also become concerned with watching the growth and activities of international terrorist organizations. The information gathered about these groups is vital to the safety of American military and foreign service personnel.

The CIA monitors these same areas, but its efforts are not focused on foreign military affairs. This organization is more concerned with the political and social situations in other countries. It does not make decisions on how the United States government should react to international events, but provides information to those officials who do set national policy.

The job of the intelligence analyst in either agency is to gather all bits of information, which may be fragmentary or secondhand, and to try to create a coherent image of a nation or a particular international problem.

The historian's skills are needed to analyze the political, historical, cultural, and social institutions of other nations. You examine the evolution of a nation, seeing how the trends and precedents of the past relate to the present a future.

In many jobs the ability to speak or read a foreign language is a valuable asset. For example, the CIA has an entire department devoted simply to following international news media. Both agencies offer opportunities to work abroad for a part of your career, but options are available only to experienced personnel.

Both agencies hire outside the Office of Personnel Management. Each subjects applicants to medical exams and stringent security checks. Many applicants have advanced degrees, but those with bachelor's degrees are considered. Each agency has an extensive training program for entry-level personnel.

At the entry level, you are responsible for gathering information from various sources. The more advanced you become, the more you will be involved in analysis. Continuing education is an important part of any intelligence career. Your agency will offer classes that will increase your knowledge and expertise, and you may be required to study at a university or college.

For information on careers in the CIA, write:
   Director of Personnel
   Central Intelligence Agency
   Washington, DC 20505

For information on careers with the DIA, write:
   Defense Intelligence Agency
   Civilian Personnel Operation Division

   Recruitment Office
   Washington, DC 20301

FOREIGN SERVICE

The foreign service serves the President and the Secretary of State by planning and conducting United States foreign policy. Foreign Service officers (FSO) work at the State Department in Washington, DC, and in over 230 embassies, missions, and consulates around the world. The foreign service offers an unusually varied career, but the decision to explore this department should not be taken lightly. You will be successful and happy only if you have extraordinary discipline and commitment, and view the benefits as far outweighing the sacrifices.

The foreign service is among the most competitive careers you might explore. Simply getting an offer of a foreign service commission is difficult; throughout a life of service, you can expect to compete against other skilled FSOs for virtually every assignment and promotion.

Obviously, only United States citizens are eligible. You must first sit for the foreign service exam, offered the first Saturday of each December. A broad knowledge of domestic and foreign affairs, with an emphasis on American history, government and culture, is required. English skills are tested, because an FSO must articulate United States policies. A test of specific skill areas determines the elements of foreign service work best suited to your abilities.

If you pass the test, you are given an all-day oral assessment of your background, temperament, and attitudes. Finally, you must pass a medical exam. With these requirements successfully completed, you are placed on one or more registers, depending on your skills and interests. Each register leads to placement in one of five functional areas: political, economic, administrative, consular, and informational-cultural. The number of openings varies from year to year, but of the approximately 12,000 people who take the test each December, perhaps 300 will eventually be commissioned. The majority of appointees have advanced degrees or work experience or both; their maturity and increased knowledge make the competition even tougher for recent graduates.

If you are accepted into the foreign service, you are given several weeks of orientation at the Foreign Service Institute, followed by up to seven months of training. Fluency in a foreign language is not a requirement for application, but it is an asset. FSOs are instructed in a language, and the length of your training is largely determined by your needs in this area.Your career prospects are enhanced by competence in several languages. The foreign service is particularly interested in applicants who speak Russian, Arabic, Mandarin Chinese, and other languages rarely studied by Americans.

Sixty percent of the average FSO career is spent abroad, and an important prerequisite for application is a willingness to be assigned anywhere. You may be pleased at the thought of working in Hong Kong or Brussels, but how do you feel about Ouagadougou, Port Moresby, and Tegucigalpa? In many parts of the world, respect for diplomatic immunity can no longer be taken for granted, and the threat of international terrorism is forcing embassies to adopt once-unimagined security measures. Personal safety has become an important consideration, especially for officers with families. Regardless of the capacity in which you serve, the most important part of your job is defending and winning support for United States policies, even those contrary to your personal opinions.

There are five principal areas in which you may serve:

POLITICAL AFFAIRS: As a political officer, you analyze the political situation in the country to which you are posted, and present United States policies to officials of that nation's government. In Washington, DC, political officers serve in State Department offices that specialize in various regions. They analyze embassy reports, brief government officials, and work with foreign diplomats accredited to Washington.

ECONOMIC AFFAIRS: Economic officers stationed abroad interpret United States economic policies while analyzing and reporting on foreign economies. To understand a nation's economy, the officer studies local finances, trade, resources, and industries. In Washington, DC, economic officers contribute to the formulation of national and international economic policies.

If you do well in the economic portion of the foreign service exam, you may also be considered for appointment to the Foreign Commercial Service. Here you work under the direction of the Department of Commerce rather than the Department of State. The Foreign Commercial Service Officer is stationed abroad and seeks to promote trade between the United States and a foreign nation. The job involves a great deal of work with local business and government officials, so language skills are extremely important.

ADMINISTRATIVE AFFAIRS: Overseas, administrative officers are concerned with daily operations of embassies and consulates, such as personnel, budgeting, security, and communications. In Washington, DC, they provide support for those stationed abroad.

CONSULAR SERVICES: Here you work closely with the public, both American citizens and foreign nationals, by dealing with passport, visa, and immigration concerns. Foreign language skills are extremely important. Consular officers are stationed in embassies and consulates, which are located in key foreign cities. In Washington, DC, the Bureau of Consular Affairs provides support for consular officers abroad with guidance and aid in problem situations.

UNITED STATES INTERNATIONAL COMMUNICATION AGEN-
CY: This agency strives to give foreign people an understanding
of American culture, attitudes, institutions, and values. Service as
a foreign service information officer means getting to know a
foreign society while explaining our own by importing and dis-
seminating American art, films, and journalism. You might also
be involved in organizing educational and cultural exchange programs. An important part of your job will be to invite American
lecturers, performers, and athletes to visit the country in which you
are stationed. Information officers in Washington help to coordinate these visits.

Career Paths

Your career path will vary with the changing policies and needs of
the State Department. You are reassigned at intervals of two to four
years, often alternating an overseas posting with a stay in Washington, DC. However, assignments are entirely dependent on your
skills and where they can best be used at any given time. Experienced FSOs are expected to specialize in a function, such as
political affairs or consular services. However, in practice, most
FSOs perform a variety of jobs. Officers are ranked, and promotions depend on annual ratings.

An ambassadorship is publicly perceived as the highest foreign
service post. However, in reality, most United States ambassadors
are political appointees who have little or no foreign service
experience. Some skilled FSOs reach the level of senior foreign
service officers. These may be appointed as ambassadors, but most
senior officers remain in the United States, guiding State Department policies and programs.

For information on foreign service careers, write:
    Foreign Service Management
    Officer Recruitment Branch
    P.O. Box 9317
    Rosslyn Station
    Arlington, VA 22209-0317

ADDITIONAL INFORMATION

Salaries

Although governmental bodies often pay their employees less than private industries, they offer attractive perks. Government employees receive generous vacation and sick leave, exceptional benefits, and pension and early retirement plans.

Most federal employees, including the CIA and the DIA are paid according to a standard pay schedule. Each promotion is accompanied by a change of GS rating. The typical graduate is hired as a GS-5 or GS-7, depending on academic record and work experience. A graduate degree holder is hired at GS-9. In the foreign service, the pay schedule is comparable to that in other government jobs, but varies according to the nation in which you are stationed. Foreign Service Officers in many countries receive hardship pay and/or living allowances.

The following chart gives the federal white-collar annual pay schedule as of January 1, 1984 (figures are the lowest wages for each GS rating).

GS1	$ 8,980	GS10	$23,088
GS2	$10,097	GS11	$25,366
GS3	$11,017	GS12	$30,402
GS4	$12,367	GS13	$36,152
GS5	$13,837	GS14	$42,722
GS6	$15,423	GS15	$50,252
GS7	$17,138	GS16	$58,938
GS8	$18,981	GS17	$69,042
GS9	$20,965	GS18	$80,920

Extracurricular Activities/Work Experience

Model United Nations
Student Government
Participation in a language house or organizations that
investigate other cultures

Writing for campus publications, particularly those that deal with national and international affairs

Internships

The federal government sponsors an excellent program of cooperative education for undergraduates. However, for you to be eligible, your college must participate in the program.

Students from a wide variety of majors are recruited to work full-time or part-time at a government agency. Most positions are for those with a specific academic concentration, such as accounting and computer science. Students with other backgrounds can find openings, but opportunities are more limited. For information, consult your school's internship or placement office.

The Department of State offers plenty of options for students interested in a foreign service career. You may be a summer intern, which is a paying position, or you may intern during a fall or spring semester, which is not compensated. Applications for a summer position must be submitted by the preceding November 1; applications for a fall or spring internship must be received at least six months in advance. Students must be juniors or seniors, have studied some pertinent coursework, and be willing to permit a background investigation before they are accepted.

For information, write:

Intern Coordinator
Department of State
P.O. Box 9317
Rosslyn Station
Arlington, VA 22209-0317

Recommended Reading

BOOKS

American Foreign Policy by Henry Kissinger, W.W. Norton: 1977

Caveat: Realism, Reagan and Foreign Policy by Alexander Haig, Macmillan Publishing Company: 1984

Dictatorships and Double Standards: Rationalism and Realism in Politics by Jeanne Kirkpatrick, Simon and Schuster: 1982

Hard Choices: Four Critical Years in Managing America's Foreign Policy by Cyrus Vance, Simon and Schuster: 1983

World Almanac Book of Facts, World Almanac: 1984

PERIODICALS

Department of State Bulletin (monthly), United States Department of State, Washington, DC 20520

Development Digest (quarterly), United States Department of State, Agency for International Development, United States Government Printing Office, Superintendent of Documents, Washington, DC 20402

Foreign Affairs (bimonthly), 58 East 68th Street, New York, NY 10021

Foreign Service Journal (weekly), Foreign Service Association, 2101 E Street, N.W., Washington, DC 20037

Government Employee Relations Report (weekly), The Bureau of National Affairs, 1231 25th Street, Washington, DC 20037

State (monthly), United States Department of State, United States Government Printing Office, Superintendent of Documents, Washington, DC 20402

Professional Associations

American Council of Voluntary Agencies for Foreign
    Service
200 Park Avenue South
New York, NY 10003

American Foreign Policy Institute
1101 17th Street, N.W.
Suite 1000
Washington, DC 20036

National Committee on American Foreign Policy
200 Park Avenue
Suite 4416
New York, NY 10017

INTERVIEWS

Edwin Jorge
Recruiter and Former Volunteer
Peace Corps, New York, NY

Before I joined the Peace Corps, I had worked my way up to vice president of a nonprofit organization that dealt with economic development for minorities. I had been aware of the Peace Corps since its inception, and in 1979 I decided that I was financially secure enough to leave my job and become a volunteer.

Because I was born in the Caribbean, I wanted to be posted to that part of the world. I was sent to Jamaica as a community development specialist. I went with the intention of doing something to help the children of Jamaica. I started off with $2000 in seed money from the Canadian government and with it I started programs to get delinquent boys off the streets. We taught them math and English and eventually started a vocational program in auto mechanics. The Street Corner Boys' Program, as it was called, grew to include a medical and dental program and, finally, a hot lunch program. In addition to the Canadian donation, I received funds from the Dutch Government and some Norwegian expatriates, and the assistance of Mitzi Seaga, the wife of the Prime Minister. By the time I left Kingston, that initial $2000 had grown to a total operating budget of over $150,000, including gifts-in-kind. I enjoyed my work and was satisfied that I had accomplished a lot of what I had set out to do. As far as I know, these programs are still operating.

When I finished my two years, I knew I wanted to stay with the Peace Corps and that I wanted to recruit. I felt I had a good idea of what makes a good volunteer, and I wanted to contribute to the Corps by ensuring that only the best people are sent abroad. Because of what I had accomplished in Kingston, I was given an excellent recommendation and moved directly into recruiting.

I interview candidates and decide if they have what it takes to be volunteers. A recruiter has to be an excellent judge of character, because there is no lack of applicants. Each candidate is assigned to a recruiter. If I get someone who is well-qualified, it is my responsibility to get that person to make a commitment and volunteer.

We are especially interested in finding people who have been involved in the community. We also like to see some demonstrated interest in the Third World, but that is not an absolute requirement. The key to being accepted is proving that you want to work with people and that you will be able to live in another culture.

To be quite honest, the Peace Corps is the best job I've ever had. I love it. When I made the decision to become a recruiter, I took a cut in salary that left me with half of what I was making when I went into the Corps as a volunteer. I wouldn't change that decision for anything.

Stephanie Smith Kinney, Age 40
Foreign Service Officer; Uruguay/Paraguay Desk, Bureau of
Inter-American Affairs
Department of State, Washington, DC

My interest in the foreign service goes back a long way. I first investigated it in high school and my research had discouraging results. At that time, I discovered, a foreign service career was difficult for women. Female officers did not go beyond mid-level positions, married women weren't accepted, and if a female officer married, an unwritten rule compelled her to resign.

But I kept my long-standing interest in the rest of the world. At Vassar, I majored in Spanish literature and Latin American affairs. I spent my junior year at the University of Madrid. I was interested in teaching, so I went on for a master's in education at Harvard.

The foreign service reentered my life when my husband became a foreign service officer about a year after we were married. His first assignment was Mexico City, which he accepted at my instigation. I wanted to be in a Spanish-speaking country because I thought I could use my background. I experienced the difficulty of being a foreign service spouse when I found that restrictions prevented me from working. I fought the regulations and became the first United States foreign service spouse officially permitted to work in Mexico City.

When we returned to Washington in 1974 we were faced with a choice: sacrifice my desire for a career, my husband's career, or our marriage. I decided the easiest option was to try to change the system in which my husband worked. I became part of a group that was working to get the State Department to be more concerned with the problems of foreign service spouses and families.

I finally decided that the best way to fight the foreign service was to join it (married women were no longer excluded), and I passed the exam and the orals and was accepted as an officer in 1976. One of my first assignments was as a management analyst charged with looking into family issues and "solving the growing spouse problems." I was a key force in creating the Family Liaison Office, the headquarters of which was inaugurated in the State Department in

March 1977. Today, it has 92 branches overseas, which help family members deal with the myriad problems posed by their highly mobile, international life-style.

From that start I've done a variety of things. I'm in the administrative function or "cone," but I've never had a truly administrative job. Now I'm on a political desk, Uruguay and Paraguay. Before that, I was with the United States Information Agency in New York. I served as assistant science attaché and also did consular and press work in Rome, and I worked in cultural affairs for West Africa in the Department.

The best and the most successful people rarely conform to structure—if you're creative, you cut your own path. My own career has been a combination of coincidence and necessity. My husband and I try to coordinate our assignments, but we must always apply individually. If a couple is not given assignments at the same post, they may take separate assignments or one spouse may take leave without pay.

If you are considering a career in the foreign service, you must be a generalist: have a background in American culture and history, economics, public administration, and political analysis. You should be confident that you can learn a foreign language. Some experience abroad is an asset—if only because it proves you can work in another culture. You must have a sense of conviction about the United States—a sense of what we are and what we should be—and a willingness to serve it. On the personal side, you must have social graces (or a willingness to learn them), a high tolerance for frustration, a sense of adventure, optimism, and a sense of humor. Although you play a defined role in a tradition-bound profession, what enables you to perform is your own sense of purpose.

It is important that you think through your priorities and your needs as a person. What do you want in a career? Do you want marriage? Children? It is difficult enough to combine a family and a career when you stay in one place—it's that much more difficult in a highly mobile career. People often see only the glamour and excitement of foreign service life—to the exclusion of the drudgery, danger, and sacrifice it can also require. It's not just a job, it's a total commitment—so it's better not to approach it with any illusions.

HUMAN SERVICES

A constellation of diverse occupations grouped under the general heading of human services presents a wide choice for those graduates who have a special feeling for working with people. Patience, sincere interest in others, a caring attitude, and a real desire to help the less fortunate are necessary conditions for these jobs—but they are not sufficient ones. A constructive tough-mindedness is equally imperative. Along with the satisfaction of seeing tangible results and of being able to effect positive changes in the lives of those in trouble come frustrations of all sorts: the daily encounter with personal tragedies; the discouraging effort to make even a small dent in seemingly intractable social problems. But if you are equipped to maintain the necessary precarious balance, a career in one of the helping professions, as they are often called, may well be for you.

Your college studies have given you some understanding of the diversity of human interaction and the consequences of an individual's inability to function. But undergraduate training only lays the groundwork for a career in human services. Advanced degrees, such as a master's in social work or occupational therapy, or a doctorate or credentials for certain specialties, such as counseling alcoholics, are not only required for advancement, but are needed for many entry-level jobs. Although there are employers who will hire job candidates with only a bachelor's degree, your career prospects will become severely limited if you do not augment your education and training.

The types of jobs you might be offered if you have no advanced degree vary. Some entry-level jobs can be very challenging; others are of the paraprofessional variety, and are low paying and do not always involve you in highly challenging work.

Jobs may be found in the following areas of human services:

- **Counseling**
- **Psychology Paraprofessionals**
- **Administration**
- **Advocacy**
- **Research**
- **Community Relations**
- **Program Development**

These positions are available in a wide variety of institutions and agencies. There are social service agencies in the federal, state, and local governments, and national, state, and local private nonprofit organizations as well. Coupled with private and public institutions and health care facilities, these represent a sizable job bank. However, since much of the funding for human services, both public and private, depends on the federal government, the number of jobs available and the salaries they offer vary with the political climate. At the present time there is relatively little money being invested in these services, and many institutions have been forced to cut back on their programs.

Job Outlook

Job Openings Will Grow: More slowly than average

Competition for Jobs: Keen
Graduates should realize that the human services are among the most competitive of all professions. Dedication, a solid record of academic achievement, and self-confidence are important attributes in job seekers.

New Job Opportunities: Demographic projections indicate that our population will have a higher percentage of elderly people in the decades to come. This change will produce an increased demand for geriatric care and counseling and other services for the elderly. Jobs will also be opening up in alcohol and substance abuse programs. The profession is moving away from its traditional dependence on large institutions; new jobs are going to be in small, nonconventional facilities such as halfway houses and hospices.

Many of the most difficult to fill jobs in human services require foreign language abilities. If you can converse easily in Spanish or (although less frequently required) some other language, you find more jobs open to you.

Geographic Job Index

There are jobs in government agencies and private organizations throughout the country. Many agencies and services operate in cities, but jobs are not limited to urban areas. The offices that administer many federal agencies are situated in or near Washington, DC, although the people who actually provide the services are located in every state. Because of the difficulty of finding entry-level positions, a willingness to relocate will provide you with more options.

Who the Employers Are

NATIONAL NONPROFIT ORGANIZATIONS employ people in all functional areas. In branches throughout the country, organizations such as the YMCA or the Boys' Clubs of America hire counselors, advocates, and program development staffs. These local branches also have administrative and community relations posts. Naturally there is a wider selection of administrative, research, and program development positions at national headquarters.

Most nonprofit agencies are organized around a specific social issue. For example, Goodwill Industries of America is concerned with helping the physically disabled; Planned Parenthood deals with family planning and women's reproductive freedom. Examine your own interests and beliefs and try to choose an agency whose work is important to you. You will be more effective in, and get more satisfaction from, a job you believe in.

THE FEDERAL GOVERNMENT provides most social services through the Department of Health and Human Services. Its agencies, such as the Administration on Aging, the Office of Child Development, and the Office for Handicapped Individuals, address specific social issues. The Department of Justice and the Veterans' Administration are also good sources of jobs for recent graduates. Depending on the department or agency, a wide variety of positions is available in counseling, program development, administration, and research. The major drawback to federal jobs is their sensitivity to the political climate. A change of administration can affect personnel, hiring, funding, and the fundamental goals of an agency.

STATE AND LOCAL GOVERNMENTS provide numerous jobs in all functional areas.

COMMUNITY MENTAL HEALTH FACILITIES AND HOSPITALS hire those with a B.A. degree as mental health paraprofessionals whose principal job is to assist psychologists. Substantive mental health care is provided by professional psychologists with advanced degrees.

How to Break into the Field

Practical experience is the key. A job in human services stresses interpersonal relationships and commitment, and any experience you have working with people is a plus. Look into volunteer work: you might try peer counseling at a college drop-in center, or helping out at an event such as the Special Olympics for handicapped people. Paid experience carries even more weight than volunteer work. A paid part-time or summer job in human services can help enormously in making contacts and in making a good impression on an interviewer.

Although a good résumé and cover letter may win you an interview, your performance at the interview will be the most important factor in whether you are hired. The interviewer will be assessing your interpersonal skills. Developing a rapport and confidently communicating your abilities and experience are vital skills.

To get an entry-level position with the federal government you should start at a Federal Job Information Center, which is listed under United States Government in the telephone book. These centers provide specific information on what jobs are available, which forms you must file, and whether a civil service examination is required.

For information on state employment, contact the state personnel department; for local work, the county or city personnel office.

International Job Opportunities

Although you will not be able to find a job in human services abroad, a number of options are open to you if you want to gain insights into the needs of people in other nations. The American Friends Service Committee, various church-affiliated organizations, and the Peace Corps are among the organizations that send volunteers abroad. Such programs are usually competitive—the Peace Corps is especially selective—but they take recent graduates. Such positions test your endurance, your commitment, and your ability to serve the needs of others.

COUNSELING

A counseling position allows the most direct contact with those you are trying to help. Counselors who work in crisis intervention, rehabilitation, guidance, or within a direct care facility for the mentally retarded or the physically disabled often need only a B.A. degree and some experience in counseling. They may work with clients face-to-face or via a phone-in hotline. These jobs are oriented toward solving urgent, immediate problems rather than deep psychological disabilities. They combine sympathy and understanding with practical resources that facilitate day-to-day living for those faced with a variety of problems—physical abuse, drug or alcohol addiction, or unemployment, to name a few.

Counseling work provides the emotional, intellectual and psychological benefits that result from changing people's lives for the better. Most counselors find it particularly rewarding to work with those to whom they are naturally drawn. Some prefer working with emotionally disturbed children; others find satisfaction in helping the elderly. Knowing your own predilections can make a big difference in how well you do your job and the amount of satisfaction you derive from it.

A related profession is guidance counseling, which involves working with students in schools. State certification is required; qualifications vary, but they may include advanced training, certification to teach, and, in some states, teaching experience. In addition to offering vocational advice, guidance counselors help students handle academic, social, and behavioral problems.

Qualifications:

Personal: A desire to help people on a one-to-one basis. The ability to listen to and empathize with a client. Capacity for working with other counselors.

Professional: A knowledge of social issues and problems. Writing and basic research skills. Knowledge of the resources available to counselors.

Job Responsibilities

Entry Level

THE BASICS: Talking to clients in person or on a telephone hotline. Keeping records of counseling sessions. Maintaining a referral file. Clerical duties.

MORE CHALLENGING DUTIES: Contacting and dealing with other service agencies. Handling difficult client cases. Attending staff meetings and seminars. Preparing reports, charts, and statistical records.

Moving Up

For many people who work as counselors, moving up means taking an administrative or supervisory position. Such a position would usually entail overseeing and organizing a staff of counselors.

To progress beyond that level, a counselor needs an advanced degree. Many people who have worked as counselors and administrators often go into program development and community relations. Because these functional areas are all people-oriented jobs, professionals often move among them.

PSYCHOLOGY PARAPROFESSIONAL

Although you may land a job in counseling with only a bachelor's degree, you will probably find that you are best suited to jobs that fall under such titles as mental health assistant, technician, or aide. These paraprofessional positions are usually found in institutional settings such as state hospitals, community mental health centers, facilities for the mentally retarded, or senior citizens centers. Psychology paraprofessionals work under the supervision of a professional psychologist or social worker and usually perform such duties as screening and evaluating new patients, directing patient contact activities, engaging in advocacy of patient needs, and assisting in community consultation. Or you may be assigned to a hotline, talking on the telephone to battered women, possible suicides, or victims of rape or child abuse.

Mental health paraprofessional work is low paying, generally does not carry much status, and often includes a great deal of drudge work. Nevertheless, such jobs are a source of experience and give you an opportunity to discover whether you have the desire and temperament to become a professional psychologist or social worker.

ADMINISTRATION

Administrative work requires a good sense of organization. You handle the endless details that keep a service operating smoothly. Responsibilities include everything from overseeing a staff to ordering office supplies. Administrative jobs involve little contact with the people for whom a service exists. However, because you deal with the people who work directly with the clients, you still need to be highly sensitive to the needs of others. Supportive administrators are the first line of defense in a field in which professionals often suffer emotional and physical burnout.

In many health care facilities, you need a master's degree in health care administration, but some government and nonprofit organizations do offer some administrative positions that do not require a master's degree. However, these entry-level jobs may not always involve you in highly challenging work. The most interesting jobs in human services administration often go to people with experience in counseling, advocacy, or some other area of the profession.

Qualifications

Personal: A strong sense of organization. The ability to remain calm under pressure. The skills to supervise others with tact and understanding. Sound judgment. A sense of fairness.

Professional: Typing. Management skills. Financial skills, such as basic accounting. An understanding of the type of service you will help administer.

Job Responsibilities

Entry Level

THE BASICS: Answering phones. Typing. Filing. Filling out forms and writing reports. Assisting higher-level administration.

MORE CHALLENGING DUTIES: Organizing grant proposals. Dealing with other service agencies. Offering support and guidance to front-line staff members.

Moving Up

Administrators must be keenly aware of changes, trends, and developments within the industry. Because human services facilities often have small administrative staffs, you may have to change employers in order to move into higher-level jobs.

ADVOCACY

As an advocate it is your job to bring people in need together with existing services that might help them. Advocates might guide an ex-convict back into community life, get welfare services for poor people, or find jobs for the mentally or physically disabled, or for reformed alcoholics or drug abusers. You act as a go-between, connecting people with employers, counseling services, medical services, and so on.

Advocacy requires a great deal of tact, a sense of justice, and a desire to see people treated fairly. You must competently handle a wide variety of cases—some simple, some complex—while maintaining good relationships with your contacts and support services. It takes persistence, patience, and determination—and the frustrations are many. You must learn not to feel personally responsible when, despite your hard work, results on a case are less than you had hoped for. The paperwork is voluminous and never-ending. But the results, when you achieve them, are tangible and rewarding.

Advocates work for both private and government-sponsored agencies. Like counselors, advocates may follow any number of career paths, often moving into other human services jobs.

The most recognizable advocates in the community are parole and probation officers. They help reintegrate ex-convicts into society by finding them jobs, getting them drug or alcohol counseling when needed, locating houses, and mediating contacts with other agencies. Parole and probation officers are hired by federal, state, or local governments; for many positions, you will be required to pass an exam. There will be an initial training period—in a classroom, on the job, or some combination of the two. Because these jobs are part and parcel of the bureaucracy, moving up depends as often on seniority (and sometimes even political considerations) as it does on skill.

RESEARCH

Research work offers the least amount of contact with the people who need the human services. Nevertheless, it is the foundation upon which the helping professions are built. It ensures that existing programs are working successfully and determines where new programs are needed.

Research requires strong quantitative skills and a gift for statistical analysis. It is definitely not a job for anyone with a fear of math. You also need good writing skills because once your research is completed, you will be asked to analyze and report on the results and, at higher levels, write proposals for new programs or improvements in existing ones.

The majority of research positions are found in the federal government, particularly in the Department of Health and Human Services and the National Institute of Education (a division of the

Department of Education). Innovative psychological investigations have been done by the Office of Naval Research and other federal agencies. Today, however, hiring freezes have drastically cut the number of job openings.

The future of human services research is closely related to computer technology. Research now relies heavily on the abilities of the computer to correlate facts and figures. The profession is moving toward what is known as "hard" research, that is, research that places a strong emphasis on numerical findings.

The entry-level position in research is the journeyman or woman, open to those with a college degree, some knowledge of the research subject, and a strong background in statistics and methods of testing. At this level you will compile and sort data; check facts, figures, and sources; and enter data into a data base. More challenging duties may include reading research proposals and briefings in order to contribute to brainstorming meetings and research presentations. However, to progress in any tangible way in this area you will need an advanced degree in a specialized area.

COMMUNITY RELATIONS

For any human service to have value, the people who most need it must know about it and have access to it. Community relations workers fill this vital need. By keeping lines of communication open between service organizations and the community, they make the public aware of offered services, find out the community's opinion of existing programs, and determine what the public thinks is needed for the future.

The community relations staff work closely with the organization's administration in order to ensure that services are reaching those who need them. They also see that as wide an audience as possible knows about the organization's work, so a working knowledge of public relations and publicity is a plus.

It is rare to find an entry-level position in community relations. Rather, it is an area to which people come after serving in counseling, advocacy, or administrative positions. Because much of the work involves meeting with community groups, a solid background knowledge of community problems and needs is essential. You must also be a good organizer and have the ability to bring people and ideas together.

PROGRAM DEVELOPMENT

Social service agencies cannot address the needs of their clients without carefully- and well-designed programs. This work requires creative, innovative, and farsighted people who are able to examine all aspects of a problem and devise a workable solution. Like community relations, the area of program development is not for entry-level personnel, but one you enter with experience and an advanced degree.

Program development is for team players: everyone involved with a project shares ideas and information. No one person can be expected to see all sides of a problem, so program designers must be open to suggestions, and receptive to contributions from researchers, administrators, and community relations staff. Ultimately, though, it is up to those in program development to pull all the available information together and come up with a plan of action.

Unless you communicate well, your brainchild hasn't a chance to become the program you imagined it to be. You must be able to put your ideas in writing effectively. To move from an ideal to a completed program you must be flexible and willing to revise, rework, and rewrite a proposal many times.

A good deal of reading is required to keep up with social trends, current research, and innovations in service programs. Maintaining contacts with agencies and organizations other than your own is also important. Most of all, however, you must never lose sight of your clients' needs if your work is to serve them well.

ADDITIONAL INFORMATION

Salaries

Salaries in the human services are notoriously low, especially when you consider the amount of advanced training required for many positions. Entry-level salaries in social service and mental health facilities fall between $10,000 and $17,000 per year; the salaries available to graduates without training beyond the bachelor's degree fall into the lower end of this range. Government employees, such as probation officers, earn slightly better pay.

If you do advance to positions of responsibility without getting further training, you cannot expect to earn more than $20,000 per year. The highest salaries in the field go to people with advanced degrees and a field of specialization. An experienced research development specialist, for example, may earn $35,000 per year.

Working Conditions

Hours: Working days are long in the human services. Your hours will be determined by the programs you are involved in and the types of people you serve. The most regular schedules (that is, a basic five-day work week) belong to administrative personnel and researchers. But in any of the helping professions, meetings, paperwork, and the pressures created by chronic understaffing will often require you to work evenings and weekends. You must also keep up with current developments in your field through outside reading. The burdens of the long work week fall most heavily on counselors—some feel they never leave work, but carry it at all times.

Environment: Office space is usually cramped and the office appearance is best described as functional. At the entry level your chances of having a private office are slim, but experienced people will normally have their own offices. Counselors and advocates are provided with quiet, comfortable, private areas to meet with their clients.

Workstyle: Counselors and advocates spend much of their time with clients, doing follow-up paperwork and meeting with other staff members to share experiences and discuss cases. Administrators are often at their desks and participate in frequent meetings. Although much of a researcher's day is spent in solitary work—going over printouts, writing reports, and so forth—project and strategy development are group efforts.

Travel: Travel is not usually a part of a job in the human services, but senior personnel and, less frequently, junior people may travel to conferences and conventions.

Extracurricular Activities/Work Experience

Volunteer work, summer, or part-time jobs at: college counseling services; hospitals, mental health centers, or nursing homes; local branches of national nonprofit organizations; hotlines for suicide, rape, child abuse, battered women, or other problems; church-affiliated charity organizations.

Membership in a service fraternity or sorority: Alpha Phi Alpha (fraternity), Alpha Kappa Alpha (sorority), Alpha Phi Omega (open to men and women).

Internships

Many internship opportunities exist in the human service professions. Community and social service facilities often need assistance. Because these facilities normally have limited financial resources, paid internships are difficult to find, but many programs offer academic credit. Potential sponsors are selective when choosing interns. You must demonstrate a sincere interest in the facility's services and a willingness to learn. If you are interested in working with children, you might also consider an internship at a day care center or a similar facility.

Recommended Reading

BOOKS

Directory of Agencies: U.S. Voluntary, International Voluntary, Intergovernmental, National Association of Social Workers: 1980

Employment and Unemployment in Social Work: A Study of N.A.S.W. Members by David A. Hardcastle and Arthur J. Katz, National Association of Social Workers: 1979

Helping Others by Anthony D'Augelli, et al., Brooks-Cole: 1980

National Directory of Mental Health, John Wiley and Sons: 1980

National Directory of Private Social Agencies, Croner Publications: 1983

New Careers and Roles in the Helping Professions by Robert J. Wicks, C.C. Thomas: 1979

The Social Worker Grid by Robert R. Blake, C.C. Thomas: 1979

PERIODICALS

Child Development (quarterly), University of Chicago Press, Journals Division, 5801 Ellis Avenue, Chicago, IL 60637

Child Welfare (monthly), Child Welfare League of America, 67 Irving Place, New York, NY 10003

Community Mental Health Journal (quarterly), 72 Fifth Avenue, New York, NY 10001

Corrections Magazine (bimonthly), Criminal Justice Publications, 116 West 32nd Street, New York, NY 10001

Crime and Delinquency (quarterly), National Council on Crime and Delinquency, 411 Hackensack Avenue, Hackensack, NJ 07601

Family Relations (quarterly), National Council on Family Relations, 1219 University Avenue, S.E., Minneapolis, MN 55414

The Gerontologist (bimonthly), Gerontological Society, 1835 K Street, N.W., Washington, DC 20006

Journal of Counseling Psychology (bimonthly), American Psychological Association, 1200 17th Street, N.W., Washington, DC 20036

Journal of Social Psychology (quarterly), Journal Press, 2 Commercial Street, Provincetown, MA 02657

Psychology Today (monthly), 1 Park Avenue, New York, NY 10016

Professional Associations

American Association of Mental Health Professionals in
    Corrections
c/o Veterans Administration Mental Health Center
2615 East Clinton
Fresno, CA 93703

American Family Therapy Association
2550 M Street, N.W.
Suite 275
Washington, DC 20037

American Mental Health Counselor Association
1215 Norman Hall
University of Florida
Gainesville, FL 32611

Mental Health Association
1800 North Kent Street
Rosslyn, VA 22209

National Alliance for the Mentally Ill
1234 Massachusetts Avenue, N.W.
Washington, DC 20005

National Institute of Mental Health
Department of Health and Human Services
Rockville, MD 20857

INTERVIEWS

Elizabeth Tower, Age 26
Crisis Intervention Counselor
Victims Services, New York, NY

I began crisis intervention counseling four years ago, right after I graduated from college. I have seen and heard a lot from people who feel very desperate. They are at a point in their lives where they need immediate help. For many people who call on the hotline, we are their last chance. I get an incredible amount of satisfaction from helping people to cope and, in some cases, to survive.

A lot of the calls on the hotline are from battered women. It is a tremendous social problem. Many women are too embarrassed or too scared to confide in friends or relatives. I hear heartbreaking stories, but helping a woman get out of a terrible situation makes it all worthwhile. We literally save people's lives.

You need to have a commitment to working with people. I believe that the work I do is solving social problems on a grassroots level. I can't change all the problems in our society, but I can help one person at a time, and I think that is a part of positive social change. Of course, you don't always feel totally positive about your work. It can be very emotionally draining when you become involved in other people's problems. Fortunately, counseling is a group effort: I get an enormous amount of support from the people I work with. We have all learned that you have to deal with your own frustration and limitations.

Debbie Clark, Age 28
Residence Manager
Yorkville Residence for Mentally Retarded Adults,
New York, NY

My first job in human services was working with emotionally disturbed deaf and hearing-impaired adolescents as a live-in counselor. That had to be the most exhausting job on earth. If one of the kids started acting up in the middle of the night, you couldn't just roll over and go back to sleep—you had to respond to the situation. I think that is really what human services is about—responding to a need where and when it comes up.

I majored in psychology in college and then went straight on for a master's in guidance and counseling. With that degree completed, I started working with the disturbed adolescents. I was promoted from direct care worker to supervisor. During my third year at that residence, I started a master's in social work, but only completed one year of study. I first worked with mentally retarded adults when I moved to another agency as an assistant manager of a group home, and changed jobs yet again when I came into my present position.

My present job is managing a residence for mentally retarded adults. Homes like these allow mentally retarded people to leave institutional settings and try to live more normal lives. Basically my job is to take care of everything—from scheduling the staff to ordering paper towels. I keep things running smoothly and handle any emergencies that come up. Even though my current job is not a live-in position, it certainly is a 24-hour-a-day job. I'm always available in case of an emergency.

You're probably wondering why on earth I do this. Well, the bottom line is that I truly care about these people. They have been abused and mistreated for most of their lives, and you've got to be really determined when you start fighting for people who can't fight for themselves. I am proud of the house I run; we create a caring space for people who have lived under inhuman conditions and you can see them respond to it. I don't like the long hours, but I love the way I feel about my job and myself.

LAW

THE practice of law offers a wide variety of career choices for liberal arts graduates. The long arm of the law is an apt phrase not only to describe the law's ability to deal with its violators, but also to point to the fact that the law touches each and every one of us in our daily lives. Few transactions in our complex society—even common ones such as the purchase of a home or a share of stock—are not subject to laws and regulations; skilled interpreters of these laws are in great demand. And everyday lawyer advocates in our nations's civil and criminal courts argue to protect the rights of society and of individuals, and address the fundamental questions of what is fair and just.

The research, writing, and analytical skills of the liberal arts graduate are particularly well-suited to the study and practice of law. Much of a lawyer's work entails reading documents, and then preparing a written presentation of the findings. (For those with a flair for the dramatic, the law also offers the opportunity to argue a case orally in a court.) In its essence this process is one that an English major will find familiar from reading and interpreting poems and novels; the history major will recognize the process from examining and drawing conclusions from historical documents and evidence; the political science major will draw similar parallels from the study of political trends and philosophy.

The majority of lawyers work in one of the following three areas: corporate practice, government service, or private practice. A chapter of this size can only provide the barest outlines of the opportunities available to aspiring lawyers. For this reason an entire book in this series—*Career Choices for Undergraduates Considering Law*—has been devoted to the practice of law.

Job Outlook

Job Openings Will Grow: About as fast as average

Competition for Jobs: Strong to keen

New Job Opportunities: Generally speaking, the outlook for job opportunities with corporations is excellent. Corporations have traditionally depended on private corporate law firms to handle their legal affairs. In recent years, however, many corporations are depending more heavily, and often completely, on inside counsel. The reasons for this trend are largely economic; fees charged by private firms have become so high that most corporations feel they can save money by having their own attorneys on their payroll. Although there will be fluctuations in specific industries caused by economic trends and any other events that would influence business, the general outlook should still remain favorable.

With budget restraints and the current trend toward deregulation and decentralization, there are few growth areas in government service. On the federal side, immigration law is assuming a new importance; on the state and local side, there is a need to take up the slack created by the loosening of federal controls and the decrease in federal services.

Demand for private practitioners rises and falls with national and local shifts in politics and the hot areas in law practice today are mergers and acquisitions, bankruptcy, real estate, and tax, while decreased governmental regulation has lessened the demand for lawyers in such areas as labor law, environmental law, and antitrust. Rapid-fire technological advances—in areas ranging from telecommunications to new life forms—have opened up a new world of job opportunities for lawyers with backgrounds in science and engineering.

Also look for increased job opportunities in areas involving alternatives to litigation as a means of resolving disputes. Current trends include neighborhood justice centers and divorce mediation. The growth in prepaid legal care plans will require increased numbers of specialists to deal with new problems involving such areas as Social Security and worker's compensation.

Geographic Job Index

Work as a lawyer can be found in virtually every city or town in the United States. The most prestigious private firms and largest corporations are naturally located in or near large cities. Work for the federal government is concentrated in Washington, DC, although many U.S. agencies maintain offices in other large population centers. There is a United States Attorney in every state of the union, as well as in Puerto Rico, Guam and the Virgin Islands. State government employment is most often found in the state capital or in the state's largest cities.

Major Employers

CORPORATIONS hire in-house counsel to handle contracts, stock offerings, real estate transactions, labor relations, compliance with government regulations, and any other corporate business for which a lawyer's training is necessary.

GOVERNMENT, state and local—need lawyers to conduct both civil and criminal procedures on their behalf.

firms do not adhere to established timetables. Getting hired is often a matter of making the right contacts and being in the right place at the right time. The hiring criteria are different, too; many of these firms view academic performance as much less important than personality and street smarts.

CORPORATE PRACTICE

Attorneys who work for corporations may wear almost as many hats as their counterparts in private practice. Depending on the size and major business of a corporation, the corporate attorney would be a generalist, coordinating the activities of in-house and outside specialists in many areas of law, or might spend his or her entire career practicing in a highly specialized area of the law.

Areas of specialization for corporate attorneys might include antitrust law, consumer issues, environmental/energy issues, government contracts, government relations, insurance, international law, litigation, personnel/labor relations, product liability, real estate, securities and finance, or tax.

Whether a generalist or a specialist, the corporate attorney does a lot of business planning with the employer. This is different from the practice of a private law firm, where the emphasis is on solving legal problems. The corporate attorney attempts to help the employer plan the affairs of the company so that problems do not arise and the goals of the corporation are achieved in a lawful manner.

Most large corporations do not require specific undergraduate or law school curricula from applicants to their law departments. However, in many cases a business degree or some business background is helpful. Depending on the business of the corporation or the concerns of a specific division in a large law department, a technical undergraduate degree may be required. These would typically include the various areas of engineering and science, and are especially important for an attorney involved in patent law.

Qualifications

Personal: A logical mind. A high moral character. The ability to get along with and work well with others. Tolerance for the sometimes bothersome bureaucratic procedures that are inherent to corporate practice.

Professional: A doctorate of jurisprudence. A license in the state or states in which you will practice. Any additional degrees or training required to follow a particular specialty, such as technical undergraduate degrees for patent law. A firm grasp of the fundamental principles of the law and professional ethics. Excellent research and writing skills.

Career Paths

Although it is impossible to generalize about career paths in corporations, many large law departments do have very structured paths which attorneys are expected to follow. This would usually begin with some sort of training program for one or more years, which gives the attorney an opportunity to become accustomed to the corporation's business procedures and to learn about the various activities of the law department. Work would be done in several areas of law under some supervision. The attorney could then expect to move into a particular area of specialty within the law department and gradually progress to higher levels of responsibility, perhaps including a supervisory position.

In smaller law departments, one might expect a less formal training or introductory period, and greater responsibility from the beginning. There would also be less opportunity to move into a higher position in a smaller corporation. Both small and large corporations sometimes offer attorneys the opportunity to move out of the law department and into other areas, such as planning, sales, or management. In such cases the opportunities often depend on the interests and initiative of the attorney.

PRIVATE LAW FIRMS employ lawyers to deal with individual and corporate clients in every conceivable area of law.

How to Break Into the Field

CORPORATE LAW

All large corporate law departments have organized procedures for recruiting, and most will interview at law schools. Smaller corporations sometimes interview on campus, but will more frequently advertise openings. The smaller the law department, the more likely it is that the employer will prefer attorneys with experience. However, there is a definite trend toward hiring new people directly from law schools. Students should be alert for these opportunities, particularly in businesses experiencing rapid growth. Anyone interested in working for a corporation should not wait for announcements of openings but should do research on possible employers and contact them directly by sending to the head of the law department a résumé and a cover letter that includes the reasons for your interest in the firm.

GOVERNMENT SERVICE

Some federal government departments and agencies interview on campus, although recruiting visits have been cut back in recent years. Other departments, including the Department of Justice, require that an application be submitted. Candidates in whom there is interest are then asked to come in for an interview at regional offices throughout the country. Your law school placement office can supply more detailed information about federal hiring practices, as well as such special programs as the honors program, through which some of the most desirable entry-level positions are filled.

Many of the larger prosecutors' offices conduct interviews on law school campuses in the fall for permanent placement positions beginning the following year. For those students who do not obtain an on-campus interview or who wish to apply to an office that does not have such recruitment efforts, it is best to send a résumé and cover letter to the personnel office, the attorney in charge of hiring, or First Assistant District Attorney. Participation in a criminal law clinic is an especially valuable credential when seeking work in the area.

Some attorney general, city solicitors, and agency offices will interview on law school campuses in the fall for the following year; others may list openings with law schools as they become available. However, many state and city agencies never contact law schools but do hire attorneys at different times throughout the year. The best approach to take is to send a résumé and cover letter directly to each agency or office that interests you and then follow up with a phone call to determine whether any positions exist and the status of your application. It should be remembered that many government civil law offices, both state and local, are controlled by civil service laws. Law students and graduates interested in government careers should be careful to take the civil service exams when they are offered so that they can be ranked on the approved lists.

PRIVATE PRACTICE
There is only one sure formula for getting a job with a large corporate law firm: good grades at a prestigious law school. Large firms typically fill their openings through on-campus interviews, and they strongly prefer to hire students from those schools at which they recruit. If your school does not have a large on-campus recruiting program, a letter-writing campaign to large firms in your geographic area may net you some interviews, but only if you have superb grades or law review experience. Timing is critical, too; large firms do virtually all of their hiring during the August to November recruiting season. It is also important to begin this process during the fall of your second year of law school, because many firms fill most of their permanent openings by making offers to students who have worked for them as summer associates following their second year of law school.

Unlike large firms, which have predictable and recurring hiring needs, small firms usually hire new lawyers only occasionally, and then only when their needs are immediate. Consequently these

Job Responsibilities

Entry Level

In some very large corporate law departments, the beginning attorney's job might resemble an entry job in a large law firm. There will be little or no client contact, and a great deal of research and memo writing, possibly on a very narrow area of the law, or even on one case. However, even in large companies, most corporate jobs involve taking on a great deal of responsibility right away, including client contact as well as whatever research and writing is necessary to handle one's own caseload.

Moving Up

If an attorney stays in the law department, he or she will begin to work on more difficult and important matters, with perhaps more emphasis on business planning. There will also be responsibility for supervising the work of junior lawyers, and for hiring outside counsel when necessary, specifying the work to be done by them and examining all billing to be sure that the corporation has gotten the services it has been asked to pay for.

GOVERNMENT SERVICE

Practicing law for the government can be both a satisfying and a stimulating career choice. Government attorneys are important public servants dedicated to improving the public welfare and preserving the integrity of our judicial system. Government cases often raise challenging legal questions of constitutional dimensions as well as interesting procedural problems. The work requires an attorney who can think analytically, speak and write effectively, and research thoroughly.

With some 5000 lawyers, the U.S. Department of Justice has been described as the largest law office in the world. Its principal function is to represent the United States in court. (The day-to-day lawyering of the federal government—negotiating contracts, providing government officials with legal advice, etc.—is done by lawyers in the office of the general counsel of a department or agency.) There are 93 U.S. Attorneys who function regionally and perform the bulk of the department's litigation; their work is guided by a central staff in Washington, DC. Special case areas such as antitrust, tax, and civil rights are handled by separate divisions within the department. These are based in Washington, DC.

Other federal agencies that employ lawyers include the Securities and Exchange Commission, which monitors and enforces compliance with federal securities laws; the Federal Trade Commission, which is charged with ensuring fair market competition and consumer protection; and the Federal Reserve Board, which is involved with federal regulation of the nation's banking system.

For state and local governments, lawyers can work either in criminal prosecution or in civil law.

Prosecuting attorneys bear an important responsibility in helping to protect society and, at the same time, assuring that accused persons are given fair and impartial treatment within the criminal justice system. Their work is varied and demanding. It requires both an understanding of the procedures governing the trial of criminal matters as well as a knowledge of state or local statutory law and court precedents.

Criminal practice of this nature entails frequent appearances in court, either before a judge or a jury, to argue the legal questions that have arisen and finally to present evidence in the trial of the case. In addition, the work in a district attorney's office involves a range of other important decisions, including determining the validity of arrest procedures, assessing the factual merits of an investigation, and deciding whether to pursue a matter to trial or to bargain for a guilty plea.

State and municipal governments, because of their size and the number of services they provide, need attorneys in almost every specialty area of civil law. Housing, transportation, welfare, mental health, and family services are examples of government services, each of which is governed by its own body of laws.

Attorneys are essential to the provision of these services and to the resolution of a variety of other problems and questions, such as construction contracts, employee disputes, environmental issues, and financial arrangements.

Qualifications

Personal: Dedication to public service. Reliability. Integrity. For criminal prosecutors, the ability to deal with the consequences of criminal brutality. Ability to work well under pressure and with minimal supervision.

Professional: Knowledge of law and procedure, especially as related to the subject area of practice. Excellent writing and communications skills.

Career Paths

Some lawyers remain in government service throughout their careers; others get their early experience with the government and then move on to private or corporate practice; still others move back and forth between government service and other areas of practice.

Lawyers, like all employees who work for the federal government, are assigned a civil service grade. With promotions and continued service your grade (and the pay scale attached to it) rises. In general, promotions within the federal government will net you a wider area of responsibility, more difficult and interesting cases, and supervisory or administrative positions. Lawyers who wish to leave federal employment find that their skills and experience are applicable to private or corporate practice.

There are attorneys who chose to do prosecutorial work for most of their careers and there are others who leave the district attorneys' offices after several years. The litigation experience acquired in a prosecutor's office provides an excellent background for any other litigation or criminal justice position. Many attorneys apply the experience they have gained to the private practice of law.

Those who hold civil law jobs for state or local governments can move into agencies with wider scope, or into supervisory or administrative positions. Those who choose to leave find that their experience is well-respected by the private sector; many attorneys are able to secure positions with law firms and corporations.

Job Responsibilities

Entry Level

THE BASICS: Legal research. Familiarizing yourself with cases and issues. Drafting briefs and memorandums.

MORE CHALLENGING DUTIES: Discussing approaches to a case with other attorneys. Taking depositions. Preparing witnesses. Court appearances. Responding to inquiries from other attorneys, legal employees, or the public.

Moving Up

The competence you display in the performance of your duties is the key to advancement. But winning cases or decisions is not the only thing that counts in the public sector. You must also understand the goals of your agency or division and must work not only toward the successful resolution of your own assignments, but toward the overall achievement of your group.

PRIVATE PRACTICE

The private practice of law offers an exceedingly wide range of career opportunities. No other profession encompasses a greater variety of work experiences than may be found in our country's 168,000 legal establishments—a term that includes small general practice firms, large multi-office firms, and every type and size in between. Such diversity defies generalization, except in the broadest sense; however, private law practice as a whole is clearly a

OTHER AREAS OF PRACTICE

There are three additional major areas of practice that lawyers may choose: politics, public interest law, and teaching.

Jobs in politics include lobbying and legislative positions. An experienced lawyer may choose to run for political office.

Lobbyists are responsible for presenting the positions of the client they represent—which may be a corporation, a trade or professional association, or a public interest advocacy group—to legislative and regulatory bodies, and to government executive departments at federal, state, and even local levels. Successful lobbyists are gregarious and have high energy and enthusiasm. It is a hectic job, sometimes conducted literally in the lobby of a legislative body. A lobbyist must be informed and articulate on the issues in question, and persuasive in presentation—both oral and written—of the client's point of view.

For those with a keen interest in the legislative process, positions on the staffs of legislators and legislative committees are available in Washington, DC, and in the 50 state capitals, as well as with elected officials in the nation's largest cities. The work includes researching and drafting legislation, and dealing with outside lobbyists who may be trying to influence your legislator. If you work for an individual legislator, you may also handle legislative aspects of constituent questions and draft the technical portions of newsletters for the home or state district, as well as advise the legislator on legal issues. Work on a committee is similar, but limited, of course, to the specialized area of the committee's work.

Public interest lawyers represent indigent persons in civil matters, defend indigent persons accused of a crime, or work for one of the many public interest groups that seek to advance their special interests through the legal process.

The Legal Aid Society and the Legal Services Corporation provide lawyers for persons unable to afford counsel to represent them in family and divorce matters, child support claims, probate and other civil matters. Similarly, public defenders—who may be hired by the local government or for whose services local government may contract through a private agency such as the Legal Aid Society—fulfill the obligation of government to provide an attorney for every person charged with a criminal offense, regardless of ability to pay. Lawyers who choose either of these areas of practice must have a willingness to be overworked and underpaid; there are always more cases than lawyers. And the lawyer's need to see justice done must be strong enough to overcome the sheer quantity of human trouble and misery with which he or she must come into contact.

Those who work for public interest groups such as the NAACP, the Sierra Club Legal Defense Fund, and others, spend their time advancing the interests of their group through lobbying, arguing high-impact test litigation, or advising advocates of their group on the legal aspects of their group's aims. Positions with these groups are at a premium, but showing an interest early through volunteer work can help the beginning lawyers find positions that will enable them to work for causes in which they believe.

Teaching is an area that lawyers come to after they have had some experience in private or corporate practice, or with government. As a rule, no special degrees are required beyond the J.D. (Juris Doctor) that is conferred on all law school graduates, although teachers frequently hold an LL.M. (Master of Legal Letters) degree in a specialty area, such as tax or antitrust law. A commitment to the philosophy of the law, to legal education, and to academic research is necessary to make a successful career in teaching. Many teachers, even those with full-time positions, continue to do some outside legal work, either performing services for government or establishing a relationship with a private law firm.

ADDITIONAL INFORMATION

Salaries

Large private practices offer the highest starting salaries for beginning associates—an average of $36,000 per year. Corporations booming business, with gross revenues increasing at a rate of more than 12 percent annually.

Significant among the reasons for this rapid growth rate are the removal of restrictions on attorney advertising; increased numbers of legal clinics and prepaid legal services plans that provide legal services to middle-income groups; and the growing complexity of the economy. These factors have also promoted increased public awareness of individual and collective rights, which in turn provides more work for more attorneys.

Most large law firms are divided into departments along practice lines such as corporate, litigation, real estate, tax, trusts and estates. New associates are usually assigned to one department immediately, but may be given the opportunity in some firms to try out work from a variety of departments before their marriage to a particular area of practice.

Small firms are the backbone of our country's legal system. They provide legal services to small businesses, as well as specialized services for many larger companies. In addition, they handle legal problems for individual clients, including real estate transactions, divorces and other domestic relations issues, estate planning and drafting of wills, personal injury actions, ad defense against criminal charges.

Qualifications

Personal: Objectivity. A high regard for precision and detail. Good organizational abilities. Empathy. Ability to think on your feet and speak well. Physical and mental stamina. Ability to be a team player.

Professional: Excellent legal research and writing skills. Finely honed analytical skills. Counseling and negotiating skills.

Career Paths

In private practice you are either an associate or a partner. An associate is an employee; a partner is a part-owner of the firm. Because of increasing specialization, a few attorneys with in-depth knowledge in a narrow field may be designated permanent associates, but this is only an option in a few very large firms. In large firms, if you are not designated a partner in five to ten years, you are expected to find other employment. At small firms the arrangements are much less hierarchical, and the competition for partnerships is less acute. After several years in private practice attorneys may opt for a corporate spot or for government service, or political or public interest work.

Job Responsibilities

Entry Level

THE BASICS: Legal research and writing. Large firms: rotation through departments, or work on narrow aspects of large cases. Small firms: some client contact from the beginning.

MORE CHALLENGING DUTIES: Large firms: some client contact; responsibility for small cases and projects in their entirety or for more complex aspects of large cases; less structured assignments. Small firms—involvement in all phases of the litigation process.

Moving Up

There is no magic pathway to partnership in a large firm. However, hard work, the ability to get along well with clients and to bring in new ones, and the firm's needs in the associate's area of expertise are all key components. Upward mobility does not cease once an associate becomes a partner, although there are no subsequent title designations to denote prominence. In general, those partners who are responsible for the firm's biggest clients and the most lucrative areas of practice have the strongest voice in firm management and receive the largest shares of the firm's profits.

Opportunities for upward mobility in small firms vary considerably, so it is important for the beginning associate to assess the firm structurally to determine the long-range prospects. Nearly all small firms place great emphasis on a person's ability to bring in new business; in many, a substantial client base is a prerequisite to partnership.

offer the next highest wages, with an average starting wage of
$33,000 per year. In government service a beginning lawyer can
expect to earn from $20,000 to $25,000 annually. In public interest
work and some legislative positions, salaries can be quite low, in
the $12,000 to $15,000 per year range.

Working Conditions

Hours: All lawyers work long hours—45 to 50 hours per week is
common. Lawyers with large private practice firms, however,
often put in much longer hours. In all legal work there will be peak
periods—when an important case is being readied for trial, or
when a business is negotiating an important contract or merger.

Environment: A lawyer's office can be anything from a hand-
somely appointed private office in an exclusive building to a
battered desk and a chair in a legal clinic in a poor neighborhood.
Most lawyers, however, will have surroundings that fall some-
where between these two extremes.

Workstyle: Your workstyle will depend largely on your job.
Some lawyers spend most of their time in research and writing,
others (such as public defenders) in court, others conferring with
clients and other lawyers.

Travel: Travel can vary considerably, but in general it is reserved for more experienced lawyers. A corporate lawyer may be
sent to other branches of the company to investigate a series of
contracts; lawyers for the federal government may travel to another
part of the country to interview witnesses in a case, but a great deal
of travel for a beginning lawyer is unusual.

Internships

You will find internships available for nearly every area of law.
Many are paying jobs, others offer school credit, still others are
volunteer positions. The best place to find out about opportunities
is through your law school placement office. If no formal intern-

ships exist in the area of your interest, the placement officers may be able to point you in the right direction. Any work experience you are able to garner will help you in your search for full-time employment after graduation. Internships with government agencies and public interest groups tend to be on a volunteer basis. If you must earn money during the summer in order to continue your education, the financial aid office may be able to assist you with finding alternative funding so that you can still get some valuable work experience.

The most formal internship programs exist with large private practice firms. Indeed, students who aspire to large firm practice may find offers of permanent employment difficult to obtain if they have not clerked for a large firm the previous summer. Large firms often go to great lengths to win the favor of top-ranking students.

Judicial Clerkships

Judicial clerkships represent a unique opportunity for new law school graduates to spend an additional year or two learning the law and the judicial process from an expert or scholar—the judge. A clerkship is a mutually beneficial arrangement. The clerk has the opportunity to work one-to-one with and to learn from this scholar, and at the same time to refine basic legal skills. The judge has an eager, bright, articulate new graduate who not only handles the time-consuming jobs of researching points of law and writing the findings into memorandums, but who is able to discuss the issues, act as a sounding board, and play devil's advocate. At its best, a clerkship provides the opportunity to work directly with, study with, and reason with the judge, and to learn the thinking and rationale behind some very difficult decisions. It is an opportunity for a new attorney to get the best possible postgraduate training. Many believe that there is no greater learning experience and no better way to begin a legal career.

Federal clerkships, especially those with higher courts, are the most prestigious, but any clerkship is of immeasurable value. The work sharpens analytic skills and strenghtens writing skills by requiring you to stretch yourself to meet the demands of a sharp and experienced mentor. And it can be an incredible boost to your career. Those who have clerked will be offered plum positions, and the experience puts you into a close working relationship with people who can be important contacts throughout your career.

The competition for clerkships is intense—requiring submission not only of a résumé and school transcript, but of samples of legal writing as well. The final hurdle is the personal interview with the judge, and here chemistry and style will come into play. However, persistence and determination in finding a clerkship can pay off in a greatly enhanced legal career.

Recommended Reading

BOOKS

After Law School? Finding a Job in a Tight Market by Saul Miller, Little Brown & Company: 1978

The American Lawyer Guide to Leading Law Firms, compiled by *The American Lawyer* staff: 1983

From Law Student to Lawyer: A Career Planning Manual by Frances Utley with Gary A. Munneke, American Bar Association: 1984

Good Works: A Guide to Social Change Careers, Karen Aptakin, ed., Center for Study of Responsive Law: 1980

How to Start and Build a Law Practice, 2nd edition. by Jay G. Foonberg, American Bar Association: 1984

I'd Rather Do It Myself—How to Set Up Your Own Law Firm by Stephen Gillers, Law Journal Press: 1980

Lawyering: A Realistic Approach to Legal Practice by James C. Freund, Doubleday & Company: 1982

The Lawyer in Modern Society, 2nd edition. by Vern Countryman, Ten Finman, and Theodore J. Schneyer, Little Brown & Company: 1976

The Lawyers by Martin Mayer, Greenwood Press: 1980

Lions of the Eighties: The Inside Story of the Powerhouse Law Firms by Paul Hoffman, Doubleday & Company: 1982

The Making of a Public Profession by Frances Kahn Zemans and Victor G. Rosenblum, American Bar Foundation: 1981

Martindale-Hubbell Law Directory, Martindale-Hubbell, Inc.: revised annually

Miller's Court by Arthur Miller, Houghton Mifflin Company: 1982

Opportunities in Law Careers by Gary A. Munneke, VGM Career Horizons: 1981

The Partners by James B. Stewart, Simon and Schuster: 1983

Stating Your Case: How to Interview for a Job as a Lawyer by Joseph Ryan, West Publishing Company: 1982

The Washington Want Ads: A Guide to Legal Careers in the Federal Government, Moira K. Griffin, ed., American Bar Association: revised annually

Women in Law by Cynthia Fuchs, Anchor Press/Doubleday: 1983

PERIODICALS

The American Lawyer (monthly), AM-LAW Publishing Corporation, 205 Lexington Avenue, New York, NY 10016.

The National Law Journal (weekly), 111 Eighth Avenue, New York, NY 10011.

Student Lawyer (monthly), American Bar Association, 750 North Lake Shore Drive, Chicago, IL 60611.

Professional Associations

The American Bar Association
1155 East 60th Street
Chicago, IL 60637

National Association of Attorneys General
444 North Capitol Street, N.W.
Suite 403
Washington, DC 20001

National District Attorneys Association
708 Pendleton Street
Alexandria, VA 22134

National Legal Aid and Defenders Association
2100 M Street, N.W.
Suite 1601
Washington, DC 20037

INTERVIEW

Eugune J. Majeski, Age 66
Founding Partner
Ropers, Majeski, Kohn, Bentley, Wagner and Kane, Redwood City, CA

I started the "adventure" as the youngest lawyer in a San Francisco admiralty firm. At that time I knew absolutely nothing about admiralty law—because I had gone to school in Chicago, where there was no great emphasis on admiralty law. But the interesting thing about law is that you don't have to know the specialty in order to become a reasonably good lawyer, because you learn on the job; it's one of the last existing apprenticeship professions.

From the admiralty firm I went to another firm where I began to learn something about litigation, which is, I think, more art than law. I stayed with that firm for three years, generally working for one of the older partners. It was he who decided—30 years ago—to start our firm, and he apparently needed someone to carry his briefcase. I started in that capacity, but when there were only two of us, it was very easy for me quickly to become a "name" partner. We thought we would have a kind of small-town friendly litigation practice, but we are now a large-city litigating firm, because the large city grew around us.

Our firm is involved in all kinds of litigation, except for criminal work. I have principally tried cases in the fields of product liability, malpractice defense, and other civil areas, including actions for libel and slander. About nine out of ten civil cases are now disposed of without trial, though. You see, we have now reached the point where the underlying assumption of many judges is that litigants don't really have to use the court at all because they really should settle everything.

I think that potential lawyers should examine themselves carefully, to be sure that they really want to be a lawyer rather than that they just like the idea of being a lawyer, because the reality is quite different. You put in a lot of hours and you work hard, and you should not be misled into thinking that it's always a joyful, wonderful, exhilarating experience. It is all this, in part, but because the trial is just the tip of the iceberg, and for every day in court you probably spend ten days in preparation, you can see that a lot of the work is drudgery. And it's an even worse situation now, since most cases are now settled out of court.

The satisfaction in litigation is not so much in winning as in doing well in light of your own standards. You may have lost the case, but if you know that you lost it for a lot less than anyone else would have lost it you can be satisfied. Often you know that because of your intervention a more just result occurred. We all recall our great wins, but many other things also give us a feeling of satisfaction.

PARALEGAL PROFESSIONAL

G RADUATES eager to explore a fresh area in which to use the training and traits that have served them as liberal arts majors will welcome this exciting, relatively new career possibility. The inquisitive, analytical mind, concern for detail, and ability to communicate that earned them their degrees are precisely the traits that mark a first-rate paralegal.

The role of the paralegal, also called a legal assistant or sometimes a legal technician, remains to be clearly defined. At the moment, the broadest description of a paralegal is someone who can do everything a lawyer can do, short of arguing a case in court, giving legal advice, accepting clients, setting or accepting legal fees or making legal decisions. In other words, paralegals can do all the varied research necessary for the preparation of any legal proceeding. These duties include drafting legal documents, researching points of law, and investigating the facts of a case; each function involves processing and managing information. Some paralegals deal directly with clients and assist the attorney in court, others do all their work in the office.

The newness of the paralegal profession can be regarded as both the best and the worst thing about it. Because there is no fixed definition of a paralegal's responsibilities, you may be able to carve out your own niche as you demonstrate your abilities. On the other hand, many attorneys, using a paralegal for the first time, may tend to underrate your competence and limit you to basic, unexciting drudge work. The job description is being redefined every time another paralegal and a new employer meet.

The field has grown rapidly as lawyers have begun to recognize how the use of legal assistants improves the efficiency, economy, and availability of legal services. With the paralegal doing the groundwork, the attorney is free to concentrate on developing a strategy for preparing and presenting the case. The role is necessarily a supportive one, and for that reason some people might find the job limiting. But if you are interested in the complexities of the American legal system, but not, for whatever reason, to the extent of pursuing a law degree, paralegal work might be just what you're looking for. It has also proved to be a useful position for those who are thinking about a law career but wish to delay their decision until they know more about what it involves. Many legal assistants have gone on to law school. In some instances, large law firms and corporations have provided aid toward their employees' tuition.

The greatest employment opportunities for paralegals can be found in large law firms. Close behind them are corporations with in-house legal departments, public advocacy groups, and federal and state governments. All these groups will probably employ even more paralegals in the future. The diverse nature of the work done by these employers helps to explain the difficulty in defining the paralegal's job.

In small law firms and public advocacy groups, the role of the paralegal is usually diversified. Because of the limited size and finances of these employers, a paralegal tends to do a little bit of everything. A paralegal working for the government, a large law firm, or a corporate legal department performs more specialized duties. The areas in which paralegals most often specialize include real estate, trusts and estates (inheritance law), litigation, and corporate law. Insurance companies, large banks, and real estate firms have also opened their offices to this new profession.

Sophisticated computer technology, enabling you to process and store information pertinent to a legal case, is rapidly taking over the field. This kind of data processing is known as a computer litigation support system. A single legal case can involve many thousands of documents accumulated over months or even years. The paralegal is responsible for organizing document files, creating indexes, and categorizing data in order to facilitate information retrieval. The data are arranged and cross-referenced according to event, date, subject, individual, and other headings. As computers become increasingly affordable and their use increases, the paralegal becomes increasingly responsible for these litigation support systems. The legal documents for a single case, which once filled several filing cabinets, can now be reduced to a few floppy disks.

Whether you are seated behind your computer console or beside an attorney in a courtroom, you will quickly discover the fascination of law. Weighed against this is the limited opportunity for advancement. A paralegal in a large firm or corporation might be promoted to a managerial position supervising other paralegals. Or a paralegal may become responsible for overseeing larger and more complex cases. Other than that, the only promotions would be in terms of salary and responsibility.

If you are a bright, responsible person who enjoys the challenge of the law, you may have what it takes to be a good paralegal. The experience involving points of law and the use of legal terminology can help you enormously if you later decide to enter law school or to move into another career area.

Job Outlook

Job Openings Will Grow: Faster than average

Competition for Jobs: Keen

New Job Opportunities: At the moment, large law firms are your number one employer and thus offer a better chance for promotion to a managerial position.

Geographic Job Index

Because large firms are the biggest employers of paralegals, the greatest number of jobs will exist in the metropolitan areas where such firms are based. Corporate headquarters, however, are often located outside big cities. Small law firms are scattered all across the country, as are state and local government departments that might hire paralegals. A quick check will tell you if a corporation, law firm, or government agency in your area employs paralegals.

Who the Employers Are

LAW FIRMS with 25 or more lawyers often have a staff of paralegals. The number—from 2 to 30 or more—of legal assistants they employ depends on the firm. In a small law firm, which may consist of 1 or 2 lawyers and rarely more than 15, a single paralegal might serve the entire firm.

CORPORATE LEGAL DEPARTMENTS often have a staff of paralegals who work on such diverse assignments as trademark law, client contracts, stock option plans, employee benefit plans, labor relations, union negotiations, and compliance with government regulations.

GOVERNMENT AGENCIES also employ paralegals. The Departments of Justice, Treasury, and Defense are the largest federal employers of paralegals, although regulatory agencies often use them as well. The duties of paralegals in these positions vary depending on the agency that employs them. State and local governments are hiring more paralegals. Jobs exist in the offices of the district attorney and the attorney general; duties in these local offices are less specialized than in a federal agency and usually concentrate on criminal law.

PUBLIC SERVICE AGENCIES, such as community legal aid associations and consumer advocate agencies that help the poor, the aged, and other persons in need of legal aid, are eager to use paralegals.

These agencies often work under tight budget constraints, and using paralegals helps them keep their costs down. Paralegals in this sector have an opportunity to do a wider variety of tasks and to work more closely with clients. Many do not work directly under an attorney's supervision but instead carry out their duties independently. They sometimes represent clients at administrative hearings. Paralegals who perform such duties are called community service advisers (CSAs) or nonlawyer advocates. Because of large cutbacks in government funding, public service agencies are not doing much hiring at the time of this writing.

How to Break into the Field

Paralegal training is a valuable asset to have when looking for your first job. Courses range from intensive three-month programs to evening and weekend classes at a college or university. Faculties for such programs often include practicing attorneys, and some programs may offer concurrent internships in law offices. The American Bar Association (ABA) publishes a list of paralegal courses that it has approved. You can write to the ABA at: 1155 East 60th Street, Chicago, IL 60637. Training is not always required to land a paralegal position, because many employers feel that the most important training will come on the job. However, more and more law firms are looking for candidates with paralegal training.

Because virtually any law firm may be a potential employer, be prepared to do some exploration. Choose firms and agencies whose work suits your interests, then inquire about their paralegal needs. It is important, particularly in large organizations, to determine who is responsible for hiring paralegals before you apply.

If you would like to work in the federal government, contact a federal job information center or a branch of the Office of Personnel Management and ask for application information. Job openings are often posted at a federal job information center. For jobs with state and local government agencies, contact the appropriate personnel office.

International Job Opportunities

International positions are scarce. There are a few instances of positions with multinational corporations for those fluent in the language and law of a foreign country.

The Work

All legal proceedings depend on facts and information that can be found in documents and legal statutes, or gathered from clients, law libraries, or more technical sources, depending on the case. The organization and management of enormous amounts of information are essential to a case's success. Legal assistants investigate the facts of a case; research the appropriate laws, legal articles, and precedents; and then apprise the lawyer of the information.

Some paralegals interview clients and do trial fact analysis; they even assist at the trial itself. (Public advocates can represent clients at administrative hearings but never at a court trial.) Besides tracking down and processing all the necessary information, a paralegal must keep track of it every step of the way. (Here a computer data base comes into its own.) In addition to pretrial work, paralegals help draft contracts and mortgages.

Qualifications

Personal: Ability to write and speak clearly and concisely, and to extract pertinent facts from a large body of information. Meticulous concern for detail. Extremely well-organized.

Professional: A knowledge of law and legal terminology. Familiarity with computer data base systems is helpful.

Career Paths

LEVEL	JOB TITLE	EXPERIENCE NEEDED
Entry	Paralegal, legal assistant, or legal technician	College degree (and paralegal training)
2	Specialized or experienced paralegal	1-3 years
3	Legal administrator, or paralegal supervisor	3-6 years

Job Responsibilities

Entry Level

THE BASICS: Legal research. Drafting standardized legal documents. Creating legal files.

MORE CHALLENGING DUTIES: Assisting attorney at trial. Interviewing clients. Writing legal recommendations based on your research. Drafting legal documents.

Moving Up

With experience, you will work on more important cases and produce more complex legal research. Promotion varies with the employer. Some paralegals find that to get a better salary and more responsibility they must move to another firm. This is because the paralegal profession is so new. You have to prove to your employer what you are capable of doing and what kind of salary you are worth.

A paralegal who specializes in one area of law can usually command a higher salary. This comes with work experience and on-the-job training, although it can be backed up by a course in the specific area. Large firms and corporations that use specialized paralegals will often pay for an employee's continuing education.

Some paralegals hire themselves out to law firms on a case-by-case basis for hourly pay. Experience is a prerequisite for this kind of free-lance work, but it can be ideal work for those who need a flexible schedule or who prefer to work for themselves. Agencies placing free-lance paralegals are considered a coming trend.

ADDITIONAL INFORMATION

Salaries

A beginning paralegal can expect to earn between $13,000 and $16,000 a year, depending on the size of the employer. With experience your salary may rise to $20,000. The highest paralegal salaries—$20,000 to $25,000—are earned by paralegal supervisors in major corporation and large law firms.

Working Conditions

Hours: Most paralegals work a standard 40-hour-a-week schedule, but hours will vary according to the firm's caseload. If a major case is coming up, or if the firm's caseload is backlogged, you will probably work overtime when the lawyers do.

Environment: The physical space allotted for paralegals varies according to employer. In large law firms with a paralegal staff, it is not uncommon for three or four paralegals to share an office; this is also true in some corporate legal departments and government agencies. In smaller firms, you might be assigned a small office of your own.

Workstyle: Much of your time will be spent at a desk or in a law library. In the more up-to-date firms, you'll find yourself facing a computer terminal most of the day. Some paralegals get out of the office to attend court or to meet clients, witnesses, or representatives of their adversary in a lawsuit.

Travel: Opportunities for travel come up when a case you have researched is tried in another city. Lawyers often take their paralegals to the trial to ensure quick access to necessary information.

Extracurricular Activities/Work Experience

Debating club

Organizing campus events—public speakers, political rallies, class or schoolwide functions. Summer or part-time work for local law firms

Internships

Some students have obtained legal internships while still in college by offering a few hours a week in exchange for experience. Any experience can help you in your quest for your first job. It will also give you a better perspective on the legal profession. If you are interested in public advocacy law, offer your services to a local public service agency. These agencies, always underfunded, seek volunteers, and you would be performing a social service while you learn more about the profession. Local and state government offices offer some internships for college students.

Recommended Reading

BOOKS

Legal Assistants: Update 1981, American Bar Association: 1981

Legal Assistant's Handbook, by Thomas W. Brunner, et. al., Bureau of National Affairs: 1982
The Paralegal: A New Career by Richard Deming, Lodestar Books: 1979

Professional Associations

National Association of Legal Assistants
1420 South Utica
Tulsa, OK 74104

National Federation of Paralegal Associations
P.O. Box 1410
Ben Franklin Station
Washington, DC 20044

INTERVIEW

Patricia Duffy Mordecai, Age 34
Legal Assistant
Heller Ehrman White & McAuliffe, San Francisco, CA

I received my baccalaureate from the University of California at Santa Barbara, where I had majored in political science. I was interested in law and had taken a number of prelaw courses. A career counselor directed me to the legal assistant profession. Even though it was a new profession it seemed interesting and provided the perfect opportunity for me to determine whether I wanted to pursue law school or not.

I found my first job by going through *Martindale & Hubbell*, which is a legal directory. I wrote down the names of all the law firms that were large enough to emply legal assistants and had interesting clients. I sent them letters and enclosed my résumé. On my first job I was assigned to work on a large-scale litigation, which has turned out to be my forte. I've worked now for three firms and, for the most part, on three different cases over a ten-year period.

My second job was with a medium-size law firm that was just beginning to use legal assistants. They had hired a corporate legal assistant and I was to be the first litigation legal assistant. I thought that it would be a real challenge, and indeed it was. Shortly after I joined the firm they got an extremely large case that lasted for the three years that I was there. I went on to oversee that case and during my last year was also promoted to legal assistant coordinator. I feel that I really had an impact on designing the legal assistant program and that I proved to the firm, and a lot of doubtful attorneys, that legal assistants could be used in a positive way. It is always an uphill battle. That's one thing about this profession—you constantly have to prove yourself.

In my present job much of what I do is administrative. I oversee a legal assistant and law clerk staff that exceeds 40 people—all working on one case. I am responsible for overall case management, assist in hiring, and am the main liaison between the 30 attorneys on the case and the legal assistants and law clerks. This position allows me to demonstrate my organizational and managerial strengths.

The trial for the case I am presently managing is still a year away. I am not sure what direction my career will take when the case is over. In a large law firm I have done extremely well; however, there are not many promotions a legal assistant can look forward to. This is a concern I have had throughout my career. If firms want to keep career legal assistants, they must provide sufficient opportunities for them. I enjoy the amount of responsibility I've been given. I like the excitement it generates. It is very satisfying to manage a large team involved in complex litigation.

In large cases, or even medium-size cases, legal assistants are invaluable if they are used correctly. However, if a firm does not provide sufficient incentives for legal assistants to remain, they leave. This often has deleterious effects upon the case, the client, and the firm. All the information and training that person has acquired is lost.

Overall, however, the legal assistant profession has made many advances and continues to provide challenging career opportunities.

POLITICS

POLITICS in America is a big business. Every four years, the major political parties spend from $10 to $30 million each on the presidential campaign. To run a respectable campaign for governor or senator in the larger states takes at least $1 million. Although at times it seems only an exercise in charisma or a game of luck, politics is a highly specific and competitive field in which there are many other professionals besides the candidates who run for and win (or fail to win) office.

Over the last 25 years, politics and the media have become intimately intertwined. For the most part, the old political machine has had to make way for the "new politics": the technique of communicating a candidate's message directly to the voter without funneling it through the party organization. In response, a whole new breed of professional politicians has emerged, skilled in planning and financing mass-oriented campaigns, getting the most political mileage out of television, direct mail, and advertising.

With the arrival of the computer, the direct link between the candidate and the voter has been cemented. The computer provides the tool to create and maintain an organization that can capitalize on the image being created through the media. It allows for the breakdown of large voter lists into small, select groups; it provides a means of sending personalized letters to hundreds, even thousands of people; it monitors registration, compiles lists and information, analyzes voting patterns, and monitors membership drives.

Graduates entering the field must be interested in the political process per se, and not necessarily in the process of government. Although history, political science, and government majors have traditionally pursued political careers, journalism or communications majors and computer programmers are as likely, these days, to find openings.

There are three areas of access into the political arena: working on staff for a state or national legislator, governor, or mayor, joining a campaign, or taking a job with a public interest group or political party. Although there are many other popularly elected officials at both the state and local levels, most inherit civil service or other government staffs, and therefore do not offer comparable opportunities for the political careerist.

To break in, an internship is highly recommended. It can often serve as the stepping-stone to a paid position in a field where many entry-level employees are hired on a volunteer basis.

Movement between the three areas at all professional levels is quite common. To get ahead, you will have to develop an area of specialization, which very often entails higher education. Expertise in legislation is a route commonly taken by those with a legal bent, and requires a law degree. Other newer areas of specialization include media control, voter and legislative behavior analysis, fund raising, computer programming, and polling. Once you become a specialist, you can work for a member of Congress (or for the President) just as readily as for a public interest group or for a campaign.

Job Outlook

Job Openings Will Grow: As fast as average

Competition for Jobs: Keen

Expect the most competition at the highly visible lobby groups, which operate on small budgets and with small staffs. In Washington, DC, the representative from your home district and the senators from your home state are the most likely employers, especially if you have intern experience. In an election year, there will be less competition for jobs at political parties, activist groups, or on the campaigns of underdog candidates.

New Job Opportunities: Although both houses of Congress are limited by statute in the number of committees they may create, the number of subcommittees is not limited, and their rate of growth has averaged two per house per year since 1946. New subcommittees invariably mean more research, more issue papers, more hearings, and more jobs.

The biggest job developer, however, has been the computer. Its ability to store, sort, and selectively print reams of information has relieved volunteer staff workers on campaigns and in public interest groups from clerical work, permitting them instead to have more contact with the voters. The computer has also opened the still only partially explored realm of analysis. Its ability to index and file survey results, pertinent issue listings, correspondence records, and information on the opposition is rapidly creating new jobs for method and data analysts.

Geographic Job Index

Washington, DC, as the seat of the nation's government, provides the highest concentration of political opportunities. Senators and representatives, congressional committees and subcommittees, the political parties, and major public interest or advocacy groups all maintain offices there. Every state capital, however, acts as a mini-Washington, with its own legislature, governor, lieutenant governor, etc. State capitals also often house campaign offices for both state and national candidates. Public interest groups and political party organizations can be found all over the country, even in the smallest of towns.

Who the Employers Are

LEGISLATORS AT THE NATIONAL AND STATE LEVEL employ many staff members. Incumbent house members (in Washington, DC) are permitted up to 18 paid employees per year. Incumbent senators have a staff allowance ranging from $500,000 to $1 million per year, depending on the size of their state. This usually means a staff of between 30 and 45 employees, with up to 3 additional legislative aides employed for committee work. Majority and minority leaders at both the state and national levels maintain the largest staffs, often with offshoot staffs in various districts of their home states.

THE REPUBLICAN AND DEMOCRATIC NATIONAL COMMITTEES maintain headquarters in Washington, DC, as well as district offices in all major cities in the country and representatives in every county. The small permanent staffs in Washington, DC (approximately 50 at each headquarters) blossom during campaigns.

PUBLIC INTEREST ADVOCACY GROUPS (PARTISAN AND NON-PARTISAN) are another major employer. Among the most well-known are Common Cause, Ralph Nader's Citizen Lobby, the AFL-CIO Committee on Political Education (COPE), Business and Industry's Political Action Committee (BIPAC), the National Wildlife Federation, and the National Organization of Women (NOW).

CAMPAIGNS must employ large numbers of people. There are 435 members of the House of Representatives, 100 senators, 50 state governors, about 50 state senators in each state senate (Minnesota with 67 has the largest number), and approximately 300 state representatives per state (Hawaii with 400 has the most). There are

3047 county governments, which typically include an election commissioner, an attorney general, a tax assessor, and a county clerk. Although the magnitude and complexity of the election campaigns will vary widely with the size of the constituency, each of these is a popularly elected official who has run and won a campaign and probably hired people to help him or her do it.

How to Break into the Field

Although it might take time to become involved as a paid participant in the field, politics is one of the most accessible of all careers if you are willing to volunteer your services for a short time. Internships are particularly valuable (although not an absolute necessity) in gaining entry. As an intern you make important contacts, and you can plug into the grapevine through which you will hear about job openings. As effective is having been an active member of a public interest group or national political association. Jobs are rarely advertised except by word of mouth. College graduates who have been politically active or who have been interns hold an unqualified edge over others looking to enter the political process.

If you are without the benefit of an internship, you should write a concise and carefully thought-out letter to the legislator or political party or interest group you would like to become affiliated with and request advice and the names of anyone who might have an entry-level position to fill. Follow up with a telephone call and afterward with a thank-you note.

Use your contacts. Having good contacts is one of the keys to a successful political career, and breaking into the arena is a good time to start learning the technique. Be persistent. Press for interviews. If you do not live where the jobs are, make the effort to get there so you can meet prospective employers and members of their staffs.

International Job Opportunities

With the possible exception of foreign campaigns, international job possibilities are extremely limited. Candidates for office in

Job Responsibilities

Entry Level

THE BASICS: Answering telephones, distributing literature, filing, typing, stuffing envelopes, hanging posters, selling tickets, bag-carrying, chauffeuring, or dog-walking.

MORE CHALLENGING DUTIES: Doing basic research, attending press briefings, computer monitoring, canvassing, phone campaigning. Computer filing and indexing.

Moving Up

Doing a superior job on routine assignments will soon pay off with recruitment into the professional group from the volunteer group. It will mean more interesting work and a greater share of political activity. Volunteer for any odd jobs that come your way. Better still, make suggestions. If you wish to go into fund raising, think of ways to raise money, and volunteer to run the projects you have in mind. Pulling off a small fund-raising project will show that you can organize well and stay within a budget. Fund raisers are to political campaigns what salespeople are to business. The goal is to make more money than their colleagues. The more contributions you can induce your candidate's supporters to make, the more you will be involved in developing major fund-raising drives, deciding not only how money is raised but also how it is spent, and determining what interest groups to cater to.

Fund raising and media coverage often go hand in hand. Establishing a rapport with the press is another avenue to promotion. Press coverage is expensive. But getting it free on the news is always risky. You must learn to balance controlled (i.e., paid-for) coverage with uncontrolled (i.e., news) coverage. A media director must have a good understanding of the opponents' campaigns as well as an astute sense of how the voting audience thinks and how much of a particular kind of coverage the candidate's campaign can use.

If your skills and interest lie in writing and research, you must be able to turn out copy that is accurate, timely, succinct, and in keeping with your candidate's point of view. Depending on the campaign, research will cover local, national, or foreign affairs issues. The more your copy is used in speeches and briefings, the more your ideas will be incorporated into the candidate's policies and image.

Campaign work requires a great deal of flexibility. If the candidate you are working for drops out of the race or loses, you must be ready to step into another candidate's campaign. Job security is not the strong point of campaigning, although the contacts you make will often be good leads for finding work elsewhere.

LEGISLATIVE STAFF

The staff of an incumbent politician, whether at the city, state, or federal level, has two primary functions: keeping the politician (your boss) informed of his or her constituents' views, and developing legislation or policy to reflect those views. Every week, executive office holders and congressional and county legislators receive hundreds of letters from their constituents: some air complaints, some voice support, most offer opinions and suggestions. It is the staff's job to answer every one of these letters to ensure that the voter doesn't feel neglected or passed over, as well as to chart majority and minority views, changing opinions, and new trends.

Maintaining a list of supporters and voters is critical to the political life span of every elected official. Newsletters, questionnaires, and campaign materials are sent to various groups drawn from the list, especially to those who have initiated communication by phone or mail with the politician's office.

Partly through the dialogue of incoming and outgoing mail, and partly through testing the waters on frequent trips home, the attitudes of congressional members parallel those of their con-other countries occasionally look to experienced American campaign planners to act as consultants in running their campaigns. Foreign governments will also sometimes hire political consultants to conduct electoral referendums or design media campaigns. The use of American consultants in foreign campaigning is on the rise, but only very slowly.

CAMPAIGNING

Working on the campaign of a candidate for local, state, or national office is the most exciting way to break into the political arena. The campaign committee is responsible for all the public relations activities that establish and maintain a candidate's image. It also develops policy, raises money, and, at election time, gets out the vote.

Campaign workers, who most often start off as volunteers before moving on to paid status, are jacks-of-all-trades. The nature of the job changes to match the progress of the campaign. At the beginning, rallies, fund raisers, and picnics must be organized, the attention of the press must be caught, the personality of the candidate must be established. In the case of state-wide or national campaigns, media advance teams travel to various locations chosen for benefits or other voter-participation projects weeks before the events are scheduled to take place. Advance teams reserve the right size halls, negotiate prices, arrange accommodations and transportation, schedule media coverage, and "debug" the program of events.

Back at headquarters, direct mailings and phone campaigns help inform the public and encourage their participation, media briefings are conducted, speeches and position papers are written. In a presidential campaign with offices in every town, these tasks tend to become more specialized than in a local campaign with only a few people on the committee. As Election Day approaches, however, success for both depends on getting out the vote through door-to-door canvassing and monitoring voter turnout.

Qualifications

Personal: People oriented. Leadership qualities coupled with the ability to work well within a group. Commitment to a particular candidate or party. Energy.

Professional: Writing skills, familiarity with word processing helpful. Good phone manner. Strong sense of organization, especially under pressure. Eye for the practical.

Career Paths

LEVEL	JOB TITLE	EXPERIENCE NEEDED
Entry	Volunteer, fieldworker, staff aide	College degree
2	Assistant director of volunteers, media advance team member, area fund raiser, special interest group liaison	1-4 years (or campaigns)
3	Director of volunteers, speech writer, press secretary, media director, appointments director, district fund raiser	3-7 years
4	Finance chairperson, counsel, campaign manager	7-10+ years, (law degree for counsel)

stituencies about 75 percent of the time (the number is lower for incumbents in executive offices, such as mayors or governors). The crunch comes when a senator, representative, or other elected official casts a major vote out of keeping with the views of the constituency. In that event, a good explanation must be immediately forthcoming, and the staff must anticipate the questions and formulate the replies.

Qualifications

Personal: Enthusiasm for the ideas and strengths of a particular elected official. People oriented. Ability to work well as part of a team. Drive.

Professional: Good phone manner. Typing, filing, and other office skills, preferably some computer experience. Good grammar. Ability to write quickly and concisely.

Career Paths

LEVEL	JOB TITLE	EXPERIENCE NEEDED
Entry	Staff assistant	College degree and internship
2	Special assistant (research), Special assistant (constituency)	1-4 years
3	Legislative aide,administrative aide	3-7 years
4	Legislative director, senior analyst, press secretary	7+ years

Job Responsibilities

Entry Level

THE BASICS: Sorting mail, sending out form letters (computerized mail), compiling mailing lists, answering phones, acting as a go-for.

MORE CHALLENGING DUTIES: Answering some correspondence, following a select number of current economic and political issues, becoming acquainted with laws and procedures (in Washington, DC, this is referred to as "Hill" experience).

Moving Up

After the first year or two of working with the mail and researching specific policy issues to the point where you have become the office specialist on them, you have to make a career choice: concentrating on legislation with the goal of becoming a legislative aide (LA) or taking increasing responsibility for office management with the aim of becoming an administrative aide (AA). The first means becoming well-versed in the key issues before Congress and the current administration. Your astuteness at judging which issues are most important, and your ability to understand the mechanisms by which to get them translated into policy, or if not that, at least into gaining good political leverage and publicity, is critical to your promotion. LA's meet and negotiate with lobbyists and representatives of other special interest groups, attend committee and subcommittee sessions, write position papers and testimonies, and help formulate new bills or other legislation. To become a legislative aide, further education in law is usually required.

Many legislative employees start in the office of an elected official and work up through the ranks by moving from one official to the next as jobs open up. Others, who stay with the same elected official, will go back and forth from the office to the campaign trail. The line between legislative assistant to the incumbent, and speechwriter or policy consultant to the candidate, is often a very fine one.

As an administrative aide, you are essentially chief of staff. To move into such a position, you must show a flair for organization and an understanding of budgeting, scheduling, and constituency management. It will be your responsibility to supervise the staff and interns; to represent the legislator at various hearings, committee meetings, and community functions; and to handle media relations.

Occasionally, the assistant to a prominent politician will move into a front seat on the political scene. (Joseph Califano, President Carter's Secretary of Health, Education, and Welfare, was a case in point, having been legislative aide to Cyrus Vance at the Pentagon.) Others become lobbyists, political consultants to business, or legislative analysts.

PUBLIC INTEREST GROUP STAFF

The goal of an advocacy group, partisan or nonpartisan, is to persuade incumbent politicians to vote in favor of or against particular policies. Further, most actively campaign for candidates known to support certain ideas or positions. Usually, it is the small permanent staff that directs all the group's official activities; the mass membership can be counted on only to contribute numbers and money. This is as true of political parties as it is of nonpartisan and single-issue interest groups. All are clientele-conscious—by definition open, informal, and personalized. Lobbyists must combine political savvy with salesmanship. Staffs must carry out extensive research on current issues, assess strategy pro and con, and balance issue importance with the priorities of the administration and the legislature.

Monitoring voting patterns is one of the key activities of a special interest group. Another is membership drives. Most lobbies and political parties also publish nonprofit newsletters that keep their membership informed and involved. Staff members often develop an area of expertise: legislation, polling, field work, recruiting. In the smaller lobbies and parties, these activities are shared by one or two people. In larger ones, whole departments work on each area. In both cases the purpose is the same: to devise effective political action programs in order to bring about accommodation between the law and the citizenry.

Qualifications

Personal: Political awareness. Self-motivation. Curiosity. Diplomacy. Outgoing, sociable personality.

Professional: Ability to translate data into conclusive arguments. Writing skills. Speaking skills.

Career Paths

LEVEL	JOB TITLE	EXPERIENCE NEEDED
Entry	Research assistant, press assistant, assistant field representative	College degree (internship)
2	Legislative assistant, administrative assistant, assistant for special projects, field representative	1-4 years
3	Press secretary, editor of newsletter, projects director, field activities coordinator, deputy director of fund raising	3-7 years
4	Press director, staff director, research methods specialist, director of governmental relations, general counsel	7+ years

Job Responsibilities

Entry Level

THE BASICS: Answering phones. Filing and indexing on the computer. Photocopying, letter stuffing, acting as go-fer.

MORE CHALLENGING DUTIES: Carrying out research, becoming involved with direct mail campaigns and membership drives, mapping voting patterns.

Moving Up

The key to becoming a successful lobbyist is your ability to get the bills your interest group (or party) wants passed in the legislature. This takes a thorough knowledge of how the political system operates at the national, state, or local levels. It means getting to know key figures in both the political and private sectors who can directly affect the policies your group supports. It involves working closely with elected officials on developing legislation, working out wording, and devising amendments. The expertise this requires usually means higher education after a few years in the field: a law degree or fulfilling a masters degree in the subject area in which your interest group functions.

During the first few years that you work for a lobby or political party, you will go along on the rounds of hobnobbing with congressional aides, committee aides, and other interest group activists. You will witness, and then learn, the art of negotiating and forming coalitions.

ADDITIONAL INFORMATION

Salaries

Entry-level salaries in politics range from $12,000 to $14,000 per year. In mid-level jobs, such as a legislative aide, yearly salaries range from $30,000 to $40,000. Managers of national campaigns can earn as much as $50,000 per year.

Working Conditions

Hours: Working hours within a campaign are long and often erratic. Twelve-hour days are not uncommon. Weekends and evenings are frequently times of particularly heavy work.

It is a rare political staffer who works a 9-to-5 day. Most congressional staff will regularly work an evening or two a week. When Congress is in session, the days are all long, and Saturdays and sometimes even Sundays become regular working days. Summer hours, except perhaps during campaign years, compensate by being much shorter.

Lobby and party work hours follow both congressional and campaign time schedules. Meetings with staffers, campaign workers, or members of other interest groups often take place over breakfast or on weekends.

Environment: Campaign headquarters are extremely noisy and full of activity. No matter how much space is available, it is never enough. Count on sharing space, probably even a telephone and typewriter (or computer) with someone else. If the campaign is successful, the noise level and the frenzy at headquarters will continue to rise until Election Day.

Congressional offices, both in Washington, DC, and in the state capitals, are busy and noisy. Staff usually occupies cramped quarters. Phones ring constantly, there are frequent visitors, and there is often a great deal of movement by staff from one room to another. Politics is a people business and thrives on a great deal of interaction.

Special interest group and party offices are similarly hectic. They are often more cramped (three to five people share a room) because of a lack of funds.

Workstyle: Campaigners, depending on the team you work with, can spend most of their day out on the road canvassing, setting up programs, etc. Others remain at their desks, answering the phones and handling all incoming problems as part of the support staff.

As a congressional or special interest group staffer, you spend much of your day at your desk or in office meetings. Research will take you out to various libraries, and you will occasionally attend committee hearings. Once you have reached the level of press secretary or LA, you spend much more of your time meeting with lobbyists, party supporters and other LAs.

Travel: Campaigning, especially on an advance team, involves quite a bit of travel all over the district, state, or country. The amount varies widely, but it can reach the point where you are on the road almost constantly. Congressional staff members in Washington, DC, occasionally travel with their congressional representative, especially if they come from the same state or home district. House members are allowed 26 free round trips home each year, while senators are allotted 40. Occasionally, a representative will travel to a foreign country as a member of a fact-finding or other type of mission, and will take a select number of personal staff members along.

Public interest group staffers, especially those whose organizations operate on a national level, may travel to meet with their counterparts in other locations, or to attend conferences or conventions.

Extracurricular Activities/Work Experience

Local or national campaigns—canvassing, polling, stuffing envelopes, etc.

Campus political organizations—fund raising, writing, organizing meetings and parties

Student government—on-campus campaigning, organizing large-scale activities, negotiating

Campus publications or stringer for local paper—writing, reporting selling ad space

Community service projects—aiding permanent staff in team work, writing, initiating new projects

Internships

Each summer, hundreds of legislators, partisan and nonpartisan interest groups, the chief executive, and many government agencies and offices sponsor internship programs. Some are paid; most are not. Many internships are open to college juniors and seniors. A few are geared to graduate students with more specific training.

Most colleges and universities have internship placement offices which have access to information about specific internships. There are also a number of internship clearinghouses that match applicants with openings in a wide range of agencies.

Listings of internship program sponsors in Washington, DC, and throughout the nation are also easily available and updated each year. Besides the directories mentioned at the start of this volume (see "What's in This Book for You?") there are the following resources:

> City Volunteer Corps, Office of the Mayor
> 200 North Spring Street, Room 2200
> Los Angeles, CA 90012
> (The City Volunteer Corps places 200 interns in city
>   government each year.)

> *Guide to Government and Public Service*
> Office of Career Services and Off-Campus Learning
> Harvard University
> 54 Dunster Street
> Cambridge, MA 02138

> *Internbook* (published 3 times a year)
> Rhode Island Intern/Volunteer Consortium
> 274 Weybossett Street
> Providence, RI 02903
> (They place 300 interns in state and city government.)

> *Jobs in Social Change*
> Social and Educational Research Foundation
> 3416 Sansom St.
> Philadelphia, PA 19104

Recommended Reading

BOOKS

Both Ends of the Avenue: The Presidency, the Executive Branch, and Congress in the 1980s, Anthony King, ed., American Enterprise Institute for Public Policy Research: 1983

How to Win an Election: A Complete Guide to Running a Successful Campaign by Sandy Huseby, St. Martin's Press: 1983

How to Win Votes in the Politics of 1980 by Edward N. Costikyan, Harcourt Brace Jovanovich: 1980

Parties, Elections and Representation in the State of New York by Howard A. Scarrow, New York University Press: 1983

Women and Politics: The Visible Majority by Sandra Baxter and Majorie Lansing, University of Michigan: 1983

PERIODICALS

Congress Quarterly (quarterly), 1414 Twenty-second Street, N.W., Washington, DC 20037

Foreign Affairs (quarterly), Council on Foreign Relations, Inc., 58 East 68th Street, New York, NY 10021

Public Opinion (quarterly), Columbia University, 116th Street and Broadway, New York, NY 10027

Professional Associations

Academy of Political Science
2852 Broadway
New York, NY 10025

American Academy of Political and Social Science
3937 Chestnut Street
Philadelphia, PA 19104

American Enterprise Institute for Public Policy Research
1150 Seventh Street, N.W.
Washington, DC 20036

American Political Science Association
1527 New Hampshire Avenue, N.W.
Washington, DC 20036

Public Interest Research Group
1346 Connecticut Avenue, Room 413
Washington, DC 20036

INTERVIEWS

Susan Hattan, Age 32
Legislative Director
Office of U.S. Senator Nancy Kassebaum, Washington, DC

One summer during my college years, I worked in Washington, DC, as an intern for the representative from my district. I developed a great liking for the city and upon graduation (with a degree in political science and Spanish) I landed a job with Senator Robert Dole of my home state of Kansas.

The first position I held was that of staff assistant, helping to manage Senator Dole's mailing list. After working with the computerized mail and mailing lists, I was given the additional responsibility of answering correspondence. Next I moved from the annex with all of the machines to the main office to do correspondence work 100 percent of the time. Then, in addition to doing communications work, I was put in charge of correspondence for the entire office, determining who worked on which issues. From the overall picture of what the mail was saying I was able to keep the administrative assistant informed. From that position on I moved on to assisting with different legislative projects on an assigned basis.

During three of the four years I worked for Senator Dole, I attended graduate school at night, studying for an M.A. in American politics. It was difficult to go to school at night while working, especially in 1976 when Senator Dole ran for the vice presidency with President Gerald Ford .

My next job was with the Department of Agriculture. I was there only a year. I spent most of my time writing on many issues, so I got a good sense of what was going on in the agency.

In January 1979 I joined Senator Nancy Kassebaum's staff. It is critically important for senators to have people on their staffs from their own states. Being a Kansan, knowing Kansas, and knowing how things worked on the Hill made me an attractive candidate for the position. If you are looking for your first job, it would be wise to start by contacting members from your own state's delegation. In this way, the one advantage you have over every other person just like you looking for a job is that you know the member's state or district.

I am now the senator's legislative director (LD). The office is not highly structured; therefore, in addition to being the LD I perform functions of a legislative assistant. My main function as LD is to coordinate the office activity and to ensure that two people are not doing the same thing and that at least one person is doing everything that needs to be done. My responsibilities include giving advice and being available for people to come to and ask, "Who does this?"

I like the variety of my job. I enjoy having a number of issues to look at each day. There is no stagnation, and the activity is intoxicating sometimes. The most difficult adjustment to make is dealing with erratic and long hours. Another problem is having to deal with a lot of inflated, easily bruised egos.

My advice to college students interested in pursuing a career in politics is to become involved in local party politics, because that is where you are most likely to find out if you enjoy the environment, and where you are most likely to make contacts.

Neel Lattimore, Age 23
**Assistant to the Media Coordinator for the National Demo-
    cratic Convention**
Democratic National Committee, Washington, DC

In college I was really involved in school government. I never got involved in anything political, although campus groups like the Young Democrats did exist. I was in charge of orientation, putting together programs for incoming students. I wrote booklets and other materials, following them through from idea to finished product.

My major was radio, television, and motion picture, with an emphasis on journalism. When I graduated, I wanted to get involved in a broad spectrum of media and work with people. Although I did not have an internship in politics, I think my background, all the writing I did for orientation, really helped me get my job. Competition is pretty tough. You have to be very persistent and keep in contact with everyone you meet and interview with.

I started off as assistant to the press secretary. Mass mailings are an important aspect to any kind of work in the press department. I also work a lot with the computer, filing and logging things into it such as credentials for the press. It's pretty tedious work but it has to be done. I answer a lot of questions on the phone, I do some research, and I do a lot of footwork: photocopying and sometimes driving a visiting press secretary around town.

One of the most disappointing things about the job is that I do so little writing. In fact, many of the skills you build in college you find you don't use in your first job. You're at the bottom of the pole—you have to start from scratch. It can be very frustrating. I will look at a press release one of the press secretaries has written and I think, "I can do that." But in fact, I probably can't. Writing a press release requires a style that is short and concise and gets the point across in as few words as possible. I need more experience before I will feel that I can write a good press release.

I love the excitement and pace of the job. The atmosphere is friendly and yet really high key. One of the best things about working in politics is that you work for a specific end product. You can see what you're working toward. Who knows? Someday you might even be working for the future President of the United States.

TECHNICAL WRITING

DID you ever wonder who wrote those directions for assembling your sound system—the ones that took you hours to decipher? Anyone who has ever purchased a sophisticated piece of electronic equipment has no doubt experienced difficulty following guidelines that are a cinch for technical wizards.

In the past, when manufacturers sold computers and other complex products primarily to technically proficient clients, they didn't need to include anything beyond a manual that listed the equipment's specifications. In the age of the personal computer, however, the quality of technical writing is improving dramatically, primarily because consumers have complained, and have even based buying decisions on the ease with which they can follow the manual that accompanies a product. They want to learn how to operate equipment as quickly and as painlessly as possible, and that means clear and concise support literature.

Although technical writers have long been employed in the automotive, aerospace, precision instrument, and other industries, the computer industry has created an unprecedented need for competent technical writers. And because their work is an important component in the marketing of a company's products, their status, as generalists within a community of scientists, designers, and programmers, has improved dramatically. Because so many of the current job opportunities are in the computer industry, this section discusses those options only.

Technical writers in the computer industry write about two types of products: hardware and software. Hardware is the equipment itself and includes mainframes—the huge computers used by big business—and microcomputers, which are used by individuals in the home and the office. Software refers to the instructions that run computer programs (they're stored on tapes and floppy disks).

A career in technical writing does not require a scientific or engineering background, but it does require an excellent command of the English language and the ability to write logically, clearly, and accurately. Your research and reporting skills must also be sharp, because you must gather all the facts and concepts for your writing from the engineers, systems analysts, and programmers who develop and design the technology. Once you have gleaned the information, your job is to present it to the layperson in an accurate and highly readable manner, so the ability to grasp technical concepts and explain them in easy-to-understand terms is essential.

Technical writers have the luxury of composing and editing their work on state-of-the-art equipment. And although knowing how to use word processing software is a plus, it's not a prerequisite to landing a job. It is helpful, however, to have some experience in layout and design. Technical writers often work with the production staff, which is responsible for the look of the publication. Given the importance consumers place on being able to follow manuals easily, imaginative graphics are critical to the success of support literature.

The technical writing field is small compared to other industries covered in this book, and is growing increasingly competitive. To stand out from the crowd, prospective technical writers must have a strong interest in technology and empathy for the people for whom they'll be writing. Taking one or more computer science or science courses can help you demonstrate your ability to comprehend what you'll be writing about. Although such prior knowledge is desirable, it's not a strict necessity. Having only a limited knowledge of computers may actually sometimes be an asset rather than a liability, because you'll be able to ask the same questions users might have about the product. For many projects you must assume that your audience knows nothing, so if you are able to learn from what you write, it's a good bet your readers will, too. One of the few areas where familiarity with programming would come in handy is if you're expected to write documentation—the technical details written by programmers, and often rewritten by technical writers, that explain how a program was designed.

Job Outlook

Job Openings Will Grow: Faster than average

Competition For Jobs: Some

New Job Opportunities: Microcomputers are the big growth area, and in many instances they are replacing mainframe computers in the business market. While the economic uncertanties faced by many manufacturers of microcomputers may affect the number of new models introduced into the hardware market, the market for software continues to escalate. Integrated software (combining uses of various applications programs) is another trend that will create jobs for technical writers.

Geographic Job Index

Jobs are concentrated in the high-technology centers: California, particularly the area know as Silicon Valley near San Fransico; the Route 128 area of Boston, the North Carolina Research Triangle (Raleigh, Durham, Charlotte area); the Dallas-Fort Worth area of Texas; and the King of Prussia, PA, area near Philadelphia.

Who the Employers Are

HARWARE MAUFACTURERS include companies that are devoted exclusively to the manufacture of computer equipment as well as diversified electronics manufacturers. Many of these companies also write the software that is provided as part of an equipment package to clients and consumers.

SOFTWARE COMPANIES in the United States now number more than 7000, and more are being established all the time. Only the largest among them can afford the luxury of a full-time technical writing staff, but most of them require the assistance of technical writers, if only on a free-lance basis, to help edit and write the literature that accompanies their products. As more and more uses are found for the computer, software companies specializing in new applications will appear. Often called software publishers, these companies produce packaged software programs for micro-computers.

Major Employers

> ADP, Clifton, NJ
> Apple Computer, Cupertino, CA
> Burroughs Corporation, Detroit, MI
> Commodore International, Norristown, PA
> Computer Sciences Corporation, El Segundo, CA
> Computervision Corporation, Bedford, MA
> Cray Research, Minneapolis, MN
> Data General Corporation, Westboro, MA
> DEC, Maynard, MA
> Electronic Data Systems, Dallas, TX
> Hewlett-Packard, Palo Alto, CA
> Honeywell, Inc., Minneapolis, MN
> IBM Corporation, Armonk, NY
> SofTech, Waltham, MA
> Sperry-Univac, New York, NY
> Tandy Corporation, Fort Worth, TX
> Texas Instruments, Dallas, TX
> Wang Laboratories, Inc., Lowell, MA

How to Break into the Field

While high-tech companies don't often come to campuses to recruit technical writers, they do come to recruit computer science and electrical engineering students. If you're resourceful, you might try scheduling an appointment with representatives of companies for which you'd like to work in order to make contact with someone in the company and to find out who does the hiring in your area of interest. If that's not possible, your next best bet is to write directly to the heads of technical writing departments at companies in which you're interested. Responding to help-wanted ads in major Sunday newspapers of the geographic areas listed above and in national trade publications is another route to interviews.

Although plenty of people with communications and even liberal arts backgrounds are being hired as technical writers, an increasing number of employers prefer candidates who have taken some technical writing courses, which are becoming more and more widespread. If your school does not offer technical writing courses, consider taking some at other institutions. Many courses are offered through continuing education divisions of four-year universities. The number of schools developing certificate programs in technical writing is an indication of the growing demand for trained people. Besides familiarizing you with the process of technical writing, such programs are evidence to prospective employers that you have a serious interest in the field. Some programs offer internships as well.

Put together a portfolio of your work, including copy written or edited by you, especially pieces on scientific or technical subjects. Also include examples of technical writing that have not been published but show an employer your abilities.

WRITING AND EDITING

As a technical writer, you will be involved throughout the development of a product. You'll constantly be gathering information from engineers, programmers, and systems analysts so that you can break down a product operation into a series of small steps, find out what to do should the desired result not occur, and anticipate the kinds of problems the uninitiated may have in using the product. This fact-gathering mission can take weeks or even months.

Once you feel you thoroughly grasp how a piece of equipment or program works, you prepare an outline of the material you plan to cover in the instructions. From that you will develop a rough draft. At each stage, it's important to consult with the designers of the product to make sure that you haven't omitted an important fact or step and that the guidelines you've developed incorporate any changes in product design.

As the manuscript is developed and polished, it goes to an editor who checks style, and then back to the technical professionals for a final review for accuracy. People from the marketing and sales staff sometimes review the copy as well. Finally, the material is approved for publication by corporate management. One of the biggest challenges is being accurate in a technical sense while still writing interesting and readable copy—a process that requires many rewrites.

You may be called upon to produce copy that is not directed to the consumer. Engineers and designers sometimes need help preparing speeches or articles for magazines and journals. You might also be asked to prepare important memos or presentations intended purely for in-house use—a confidential new product proposal, for example. Such projects add variety to your work.

Editors represent only a small part of the technical writing staff. Many firms rely on free-lancers or the most experienced technical writers on staff to handle editing needs instead of hiring full-time editors. Ironically, increasingly sophisticated computer software is eliminating many of the functions performed by editors. Programs that correct spelling and basic grammar mistakes are already in use. Programs that analyze sentence construction and spot cliches are also being used on a limited basis. However, the computer will never be able to line edit, that is, to check copy for word usage, organization, and readability, so the need for editors will not entirely disappear. If you prove to be a competent writer, you may be assigned editing responsibilities, which would begin with the routine task of copy editing—checking for spelling and grammar. As you gain more experience, you will begin line editing—questioning content, clarity, and sentence structure— and assume more responsibility for the finished product.

Qualifications

Personal: Patience to work on assignments that may stretch over weeks or months. Flexibility to work on many projects at a time. Strong interpersonal skills.

Professional: Typing. Ability to break down a complicated process into logical steps. Good reporting skills. Ability to write clearly and concisely.

Career Paths

LEVEL	JOB TITLE	EXPERIENCE NEEDED
Entry	Associate	College degree
2	Technical writer	2 years
3	Senior technical writer	5 years
4	Senior editor or department manager	7-10 years

Job Responsibilities

Entry Level

THE BASICS: Proofreading other writers' work. Familiarizing yourself with the style of your company's material. Updating printed copy in need of revision.

MORE CHALLENGING DUTIES: Assisting another writer on a project. Some research and direct contact with technical experts. Learning to work on and use the company's computers.

Moving Up

For the better part of a year, you will be getting informal on-the-job training as you familiarize yourself with company products and publications and work on small projects as the opportunity arises. As you progress, you will do longer, more complicated pieces of technical writing and work on higher-status products. It's essential to keep up with what the competition is doing so that you can incorporate successful techniques into your own work. The more quickly you catch on to the technical jargon used by the professionals around you, the more contact you'll have with technical designers and management. Your progress will depend on your turning in consistently good writing and proving that you can work comfortably with people from academic backgrounds drastically different from your own. Since you're not "one of tem," you may, on occasion, have to tolerate their feelings of superiority because of your lack of technical expertise. Developing tact and diplomacy in dealing with engineers and programmers who may be extremely competent designers but poor writers is also essential.

ADDITIONAL INFORMATION

Salaries

A typical entry-level writer's salary ranges from $18,000 to $20,000 a year. Graduates with proven writing experience and an understanding of technical jargon earn more than those who require more training. Seasoned writers command anywhere from $35,000 to $60,000 a year.

Working Conditions

Hours: Basically nine to five, although overtime often can't be avoided when project deadlines are near.

Environment: The ideal situation, a private office, actually exists for some entry-level people. Others share offices or partitioned work space. A word processor is made available to every writer. The bigger the company, the more comfortable your surroundings will be.

Workstyle: The day is spent largely at your desk, but there are frequent meetings with engineers, editors, marketing personnel, or production staff members.

Travel: Some firms have divisions in different locations, requiring some technical writers to travel, especially when doing research. Extensive or overnight travel is not typically part of a technical writer's job.

Extracurricular Activities/Work Experience

Campus computer center—supervising operation, tutoring, writing instructions for machine use

College newspaper or other campus publications—writing, reporting, editing, proofreading

Society for Collegiate Journalists, Sigma Delta Chi-student member

Recommended Reading

BOOKS

Readings in Technical Writing by David C. Leonard and Peter J. McGuire, Macmillan Publishing Company: 1983

The Soul of a New Machine by Tracy Kidder, Avon Books: 1982

PERIODICALS

Computerworld (weekly), CW Communications, Inc., 375 Cochituate Road, Route 30, Framingham, MA 01701

Infoworld (weekly), Popular Computing, Inc., 530 Lytton Avenue, Palo Alto, CA 94301

Journal of the Society for Technical Communication (quarterly), Society for Technical Communication, 815 Fifteenth Street, N.W. Washington, DC 20005

Professional Association

Society for Technical Communication
815 Fifteenth Street, N.W.
Washington, DC 20005

INTERVIEWS

Betsey Babcock, Age 24
Technical Writer
Data General Corporation, Westboro, MA

My original career plans were very different from what I'm doing now. I was a music major at Wellesley College and planned to enter the field of arts management until I discovered that the salaries were low, there was no job security, and few jobs existed. Going into my senior year, I started to think about alternatives, particularly in the computer field. I had used computers before, but only to play games and do word processing, so I took several programming courses.

I sent out so many résumés to computer companies during my senior year that I suspect I must have contacted every one that ever existed! I was looking for a job in programming; I didn't even know that technical writing existed. Then Data General came to Wellesley to interview for technical writers. I interviewed because I thought I might talk my way into programming, but when I heard about the job, I decided it was tailor-made for me because I like computers and have strong writing skills.

When I started work in July 1981, I was very lucky to be assigned to a new project and to have a boss who wasn't afraid to let me work independently. We were working on an office automation project. I met with the developers, and contributed to the design of the electronic help system that users can call up if problems arise. My first project was to write the "help" messages and tie them to the proper prompts. The software also included an on-line manual, which described the system in detail for those times when the "help" messages weren't enough. It took me a year to write this manual which, when printed out, is two-and-a-- half-inches thick!

I've been lucky to get to do design work. It's unusual for a technical writer to do this, but I've developed a reputation for being good at it. The documentation is very much a part of the software, so you have to work hand-in-hand with the developers. Because of my writing, I'm sensitive to the needs of the user, and the designers with whom I work realize that that's a big plus.

I like the creativity required to get a difficult concept across to an unsophisticated audience. You really have to experiment with the right approach and the best organization to use in each project. Working out these details can be exciting.

Although I like writing, I enjoy being involved in design of the products so much that I'm thinking of going into programming— my original goal. As a writer, I sometimes find it frustrating only to be able to suggest revisions in software; programming may give me more influence over the things I want to change.

Bradley Crystal, Age 23
Writer/Editor
Apple Computer, Cupertino, CA

To me, working as a technical writer is an extension of my education. At Stanford University, where I majored in political science, I didn't explore technology as much as I would have liked to. But I've been able to do that at Apple, where I'm surrounded by innovative computer specialists who have tremendous energy and enthusiasm for their work. It's exciting to be here because I really feel that I'm on the cutting edge of technology.

The close ties between Stanford and the nearby Silicon Valley encouraged me to investigate technical writing as a career possibility. My journalism courses and working on the *Stanford Daily* as a reporter, writer, and copy editor prepared me for this job. At the paper we all used video display terminals for writing and editing, so I didn't have to learn that on the job.

Originally, I had applied to work on the *Apple Magazine* (a publication for computer owners that is no longer published), but I was hired to do technical and marketing communications writing. The challenge in my work is to present information in a way that allows the reader to understand the product and to be able to follow the directions. You must be very careful when you write, because you must assume that your readers have a low level of technical know-how.

I've written brochures directed at consumers, but recently I've been working on sales pamphlets, which we supply to dealers and retailers so they can understand our products and explain them to the public. Each is a "pep talk" on why we think our products are viable and saleable.

For a while I copy edited a lot of other writers' work, but I don't do much now. We have a separate copy editing department, but writers are often called on to edit free-lancers' work. Our department has only five writer/editors, and we can't always produce all we are expected to, so free-lancers are often used.

The engineers and designers I work with are usually very helpful. They realize that they operate on a different plane than the public at large. At times they can get bogged down in explaining technicalities and forget that consumers are overwhelmed by too much detail, but it's my job to make sure that doesn't happen. I enjoy being part of the process of educating the public about our products and persuading people that their productivity can be increased through technology.

BIBLIOGRAPHY

The College Graduate's Career Guide by Robert Ginn, Jr., Charles Scribner's Sons: 1981

College Placement Annual by the College Placement Council: revised annually (available in most campus placement offices)

The Complete Job-Search Handbook: All the Skills You Need to Get Any Job and Have a Good Time Doing It by Howard Figler, Holt, Rinehart & Winston: 1981

Consider Your Options: Business Opportunities for Liberal Arts Graduates by Christine A. Gould, Association of American Colleges: 1983 (free)

Go Hire Yourself an Employer by Richard K. Irish, Doubleday & Company: 1977

The Hidden Job Market for the 80's by Tom Jackson and Davidyne Mayleas, Times Books: 1981

Jobs for English Majors and Other Smart People by John L. Munschauer, Peterson's Guides: 1982

Job Hunting with Employment Agencies by Eve Gowdey, Barron's Educational Series: 1978

Making It Big in the City by Peggy J. Schmidt, Coward-McCann: 1983

Making It on Your First Job by Peggy J. Schmidt, Avon Books: 1981

National Directory of Addresses and Telephone Numbers, Concord Reference Books: revised annually

The National Job-Finding Guide by Heinz Uhrich and J. Robert Connor, Doubleday & Company: 1981

The Perfect Résumé by Tom Jackson, Doubleday & Company: 1981

Put Your Degree to Work: A Career Planning and Job Hunting Guide for the New Professional by Marcia R. Fox, W.W. Norton: 1979

The Student Entrepreneur's Guide by Brett M. Kingston, Ten Speed Press: 1980

What Color Is Your Parachute? A Practical Manual for Job Hunters and Career Changers by Richard N. Bolles, Ten Speed Press: 1983

Where Are the Jobs? by John D. Erdlen and Donald H. Sweet, Harcourt Brace Jovanovich: 1982

INDEX

Academic background: broadcasting, 2, 9; education, 25, 27, 29, 39; government, 44; human services, 60, 62, 63, 64, 67, 68; law, 77–78, 82, 83, 91; politics, 112, 124; technical writing, 137

Administrative positions, 13, 28, 47, 58, 64, 68, 70

Advertising, 29

Advocacy, human services, 58, 65

AFL-CIO, 114

American Field Service, 27

American Friends Service Committee, the, 61

Ambassador, 48

American Bar Association, 103

AP Radio Network, 4

Associated Press (AP), 9

Boys Club of America, 60

Breaking into the field: broadcasting, Broadcasting, 1–19

7; education, 25; government, 39; human services, 61; law, 80; paralegal, 103, politics, 112, 115; technical writing, 137

Bureau of Consular Affairs, 47

Cable television 2, 7

Campaigns, political, 114, 116, 125–126

Career advancement: broadcasting, 3, 8, 11, 13; government, 40; education, 28–29; human services, 63, 65, 67; law, 84, 89; paralegal, 101, 105; politics, 118, 121, 124; technical writing, 140

Career paths: broadcasting, 10, 27; education, 27; government, 48; human services, 66; law, 83, 88; paralegal, 105; politics, 117; technical writing, 139

Central Intelligence Agency (CIA), 43, 49

Certification: education, 25; human services, 62

Children's programs, 12

Church-affiliated institutions, 24

Civil service, 81

Community relations, 58, 63, 67

Community service advisors, 103

Competition for jobs. See job outlook

Competitive services, 40

Computers, impact of, 22–23, 67, 79, 101, 104, 111–113, 133–135

Consular services, 47

Continuing education, 24, 44, 137

Cooperative education, government, 50

Corporate practice law, 78, 79, 80, 82, 91–92; paralegals in, 100, 102

Counseling, 58, 62

Criminal law, 85

Defense Intelligence Agency, 43–45

Department heads, education, 28

Education, 21–35; consultants, 28

Employers: broadcasting, 3, 5–6; education, 24; government, 37; human services, 60; law, 79; paralegal, 102; politics, 114; technical writing, 136

Entry-level positions: broadcasting, 3, 11; education, 28; government, 39, 44; human services, 58, 59, 61, 63, 64, 65, 67; law, 80, 87; politics, 112, 118, 120; paralegal, 105–106; technical writing, 140

Experience, previous: broadcasting, 3, 7, 10, 15; education, 31; government, 49; human services, 61, 62, 68, 70; law, 93; paralegal, 105, 106, 107; politics, 117, 123, 126; technical writing, 134, 139, 141

Federal Bureau of Investigation, 39

Federal Communications Commission (FCC), 2, 12

Federal Job Information Center, 40, 61

Federal Trade Commission (FTC), 85
Foreign commercial service, 47
Foreign languages, fluency in, 27, 41, 44, 46, 47, 59
Foreign service, 38, 41, 42, 50; examinations for, 45–46; Institute of, 46; officers, 45, 46, 48, 49
Free-lancing, broadcasting, 8; paralegal, 104; technical writing, 136
Fund raising, 112, 118

Geographic job index: broadcasting, 3; education, 24; government, 39; human services, 59; law, 79; paralegal, 102; politics, 113; technical writing, 135–136
Goodwill Industries of America, 60
Government, 37–56
Government agencies, 59, 66, 78–79, 80, 92, 93, 102
Guidance counseling, 62

Halfway houses, 59
Handicapped children, 23
Hardware, computer, 134–135
Health care facilities, 58, 59
Hispanic News Service, 3
Human services, 57–75

Independent schools, 25, 29, 31–32
Independent stations, 12
Intelligence services, federal, 38, 43
Internal Revenue Service, 39
International job opportunities, 26, 41, 61, 104, 115
International radio and television, 15
Internships, 2, 7, 15, 31–32, 50, 70, 107, 112, 115, 127

Job outlook: broadcasting, 2–3, 8; education, 23; government, 38, 46; human services, 57; law, 78; paralegal, 100–101; politics, 112; technical writing, 134–135
Job responsibilities: broadcasting, 11; education, 28; human services, 63–64; law, 84, 87, 89; paralegal, 105; politics, 118, 121, 124; technical writing, 140

Judicial clerkships, 93

Labor law, 79
Law, 77–109
Legal Aid Society, 90
Legal clinics, 88
Legislative aide, 121
Legislative positions, law, 90
Legislative staff, 112, 119, 122, 124–125
Liberal arts background, 137; for law, 77; paralegal, 99
Lobbying, 112, 124–125
Local government, 37, 39, 41, 58, 90

Mainframe, computer, 134
Management positions, broadcasting, 8; education, 29; government, 37, 40
Market stations, 12
Master teacher, 28
Media, role in politics, 111, 112, 118
Mental health assistant, 63
Microcomputers, 134, 135, 136
Mutual Broadcasting System, 4

National Archives, the, 39
National Association for the Advancement of Colored People (NAACP), 91
National Association of Broadcasters, 13
National Association of Educational Broadcasters, 8
National Black Network, 3
National Council of Accreditation of Teacher Education, 25
National Education Association, 27, 29
National Institute of Education, 66–67
National Organization of Women (NOW), 114
National Public Radio, 5
Network radio, 2, 12, 13
Network television, 2, 12, 13
News media, 2, 9–12; director 11–12; documentary, department of, 8, 12; newscaster, 11; producer, 11, 12, 13; writing, 11

Nonprofit organizations, 60

Office for Handicapped Individuals, 60
Office of Naval Research, 67
Office of Personnel Management, 40, 41, 103

PACT (People and Careers in Telecommunications), 8
Paraprofessionals: human services, 58, 60, 63; legal, 99–109; public advocacy, 100, 104; public service, 102
Peace Corps, the, 27, 38, 41, 61
Placement organizations, national, 25–26
Planned Parenthood, 60
Political parties, 112, 114, 115, 125
Politics, 111–132
Polling, 112
Preschool education, 25
Prime time shows, 12
Principals, secondary schools, 28
Private nonprofit organizations, 58
Private practice law, 78, 79, 81, 82, 84, 91, 93; paralegals in, 100–103
Private schools, 24, 25
Production, broadcasting, 4, 13
Professional associations: broadcasting, 17; education, 33; government, 52; human services, 72; law, 95; paralegal, 108; politics, 128; technical writing, 142
Program development, human services, 58, 63, 68
Programming, 4; director of, 13; PBS, 5; production, 2, 12; services, 7; television, 12
Programming, computer, 135
Psychologists, 60
Public Broadcasting Service (PBS), 2
Public interest groups, 93, 112, 114, 115, 122
Public interest law, 90
Public radio, 1, 7, 8, 13
Public relations, 29
Public schools, 24, 29

Public service programming, 12
Public television, 5, 7, 13

Qualifications: broadcasting, 1, 2, 8, 9; education, 2, 7, 42; human services, 57, 62, 64–66, 68; law, 83, 87, 88; paralegal, 104; politics, 117, 120, 123; technical writing, 139

Radio, 2, 8, 10–14; markets, 4, 6; networks, 1, 4; news departments, 9; syndicators, independent, 4
Reporter, 8, 9, 11, 14, 59
Research: human services, 58, 66; politics, 119; technical writing, 134
RKO Radio Network

Salaries: broadcasting, 13; education, 22, 24, 29; government, 42, 49; human services, 58, 64, 69; law, 91; paralegal, 106; politics, 124; technical writing, 140
Securities and Exchange Commission, (SEC), 85
Soap opera, 12
Social service agencies, 58
Software, 134–136
Sports (broadcasting), 12
State government, 37, 39, 41, 45, 48; institutions of, 58
Summer jobs: broadcasting, 2; education, 28; government, 50; human services, 61

Teaching: law, 90, 91; math, 23; preschool, 24; special education, 23; teachers in business, 29. See education
Technical writing, 133–145; editing, 137–140; reporting, 134
Television, 12, 8, 9–12; commercial stations, 4; low power, 3; markets, 4; networks, 3
Training, in-house: government, 37, 42, 46; human services, 66; law, 83; paralegal, 103, 106

UNESCO, 27
United Nations, 41

United Press International, 9; audio, 4
U.S. attorneys, 79, 85
U.S. Department of Commerce, 47
U.S. Department of Defense, 39
U.S. Department of Education, 23, 67
U.S. Department of Health and
    Human Services, 60, 66
U.S. Department of Justice, 80, 84
United States embassies, 47
United States International
    Communication Agency, 48

Veterans' Administration, 60

Word processing, 134
Working conditions: broadcasting, 14;
    education, 30; human services, 69;
    law, 92; paralegal, 106; politics,
    125; technical writing, 141

Young Men's Christian Association,
    60

NOTES

NOTES

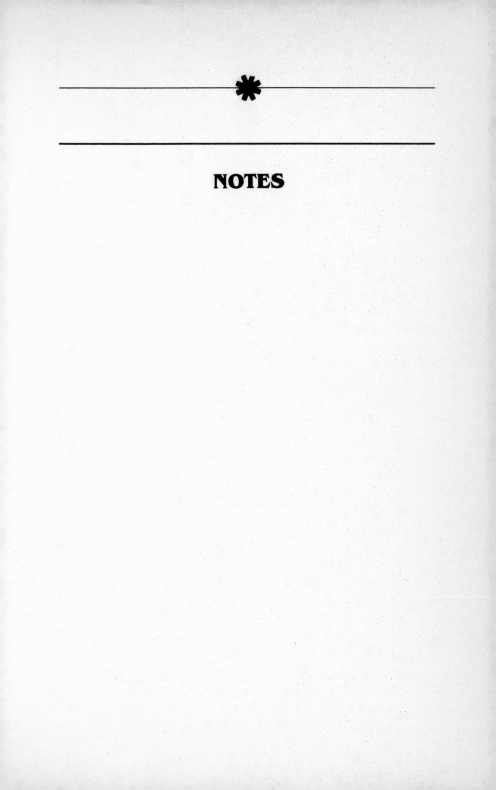

NOTES

NOTES

NOTES

NOTES

NOTES

NOTES

NOTES

NOTES

NOTES

NOTES

NOTES

NOTES